D1527747

TIER 1:
DISCOVERING SELF
"NEW WINE, OLD SKINS"

REVISED EDITION

BY:
DR. WILLIE L. MOODY JR.,MPH

Tier 1: Discovering Self
'New Wine, Old Skins' : Revised Edition

ISBN: 978-197-339529-4

Cover Image/Photographer: Crystal Glass

Cover / Interior Design:
www.NextLevelPublishing.com

centralagnewark@yahoo.com
www.chosencc.wix.com/chosengenerationcc

Next Level Publishing (Laurel, MD)

Reviews

"I struggled with Tier 1 initially because it requires diligence and discipline. I would start the process, feel better or get an answer, then go back into patterned behavior which is a set up for my demise from the enemy and the "inner me". The enemy wants you outside of the will and purpose of God. Tier 1 is a daily practice. It must be done on purpose. Like so many, I read scripture, practice praise and worship, pray sometimes, it is also why I would feel his presence sometimes, but not all the time. It is a mindset placed solely on God. Tier 1 makes you accountability to yourself because it forces you to look in the mirror at self. 2Cor 13:5-6 says to examine and test-yourself. Tier 1 doesn't allow for finger pointing. Since, you are fellowshipping with God, the God in you is speaking to the Ultimate God and Master of the universe, it requires complete submission. It does not allow for irritation, annoyance, complaining or contention. You're not allowed to be offended due to your intense focus on God. These things do not affect you due to the immersion of yourself into Tier 1. (1 Cor 13:11-13) There are different methods to staying grounded in Tier 1. For myself, I read scriptures, listen to sermons, worship by dancing and listening to music. I recommend stacking these methods because the enemy is sneaky and will slither in at any time through anyone. Just when you think you've got it together, he comes in like a thief in the night. He will use anyone to knock you off balance and away from the peace that only God can provide. The trigger could be a person on a check-out line, maybe while someone cut you off in traffic, spouse or your children. Tier 1 is "love" 1 Corinthians 13:4-7. How can you be completely immersed in God and make allowances for bad behavior such as rudeness, unforgiveness, bitterness, crankiness and so on? This is now my metric. If I feel any of the above negative behaviors mentioned, I have stepped out of Tier 1 and stepped back into self and selfishness. If my speech becomes, I feel, I deserve, I want and so on. If there is an "I" in my speech. I'm not in Tier 1. That is because Tier 1 is a practice of selflessness; it is an expression of love for God. The practice of Tier 1 keeps me balanced. Tier 1 is setting yourself apart for time with God just you and him. This is where revelation lies. It takes you behind the veil to receive answers to those questions you've been asking yourself and others, it's where you receive guidance and direction with surety. Imagine being in a relationship with someone you adore, but they only give you attention or speak to you when they want something. Parent to child, family member, friend any and all apply. I bet you'd stop taking their call if the only time you spoke with them a request was attached. God just wants a little of your time each day set aside just for him to say hello. In return, he locks those unanswered prayers, your purpose, and glimpses into your destiny and future."

-Cheryl T.

"Spiritual Warfare is real, sometimes as we journey in the flesh through this trying physical reality, we forget to take hold of our spiritual weapons to war against the enemy! Tier 1 has taught me just that, as I fought against being in an unhealthy soul tie, I had to realize I wasn't warring against flesh and just flesh alone, there was a spiritual battle taking place against my spirit, principalities in high places, trying to conquer and rule over my soul, but it wasn't until I stepped head first and put on the helmet of salvation took up the sword of the spirit that I was able to cease victory against the enemy and his sneaky malicious plot, thankful today I am being healed from that once subjugating soul tie that once had me bound."

-Brandon B.

"The learning I received from my Mentor, Dr. Willie Moody, of Chosen Generation Community Corporation ("CGCC") was invaluable.   Particularly, my spiritual growth in various areas as it related to Tier I module, "Healthy Spiritual Formation as accessed through practicing self-discipline".   For me, the essential part of Tier I touched me in the self-discipline areas of: a) prayer - it helps to keep me humble and stable, working on my inner self before I respond irrationally to others; b)solitude - I sit still and think in a quiet space - breathing in and out slowly and thanking God for all His blessings; c)giving of myself (my time) - unselfishly by remembering there are others who are more in need than I am, by first dealing with myself before I reach out to help others; and d) singing - gospel music always lifts my spirits and by sharing this gift with others once I am uplifted. This spiritual enlightening has been a blessing in all that I continue to do as I share my anointing with others."

-Chaplain Dawn B.

I want to thank Dr. Moody for teaching mental health through the Tier I process. I first began to going to Dr. Moody for marital counseling a few months ago. My wife and I were separated after 27 years of marriage and the separation devastated me. Dr. Moody introduced me to his Tier I teaching which focuses a person on who they are in Christ. And when you know who you are in Christ, you will then be able to deal with others and situations in a healthy way. Tier I also allows you to accept the consequences of life and get grounded knowing that God is in control, that nothing is happening without His knowledge, and that I will be able to handle any situation that comes up in my life. So, Tier I has helped me take the focus off of myself and putting it back on Christ. Lastly, after 4 months of separation, my wife and I will be getting back together again. Thanks Dr. Moody for teaching me Tier I concepts. It has changed my life and saved my marriage.

-James & Tara B.

Dr. Moody's Tier 1 model enabled me to reflect on self and begin the healing process for a broken spirit and broken soul. Tier 1 taught me how to take accountability for my actions without blaming others for my pain and suffering. There is no wrong in acknowledging pain, but being bound and crippled by it can be toxic. I have experienced a tremendous amount of heartache as a result of failed relationships in my life. However, learning to forgive those who have "hurt" me helped to improve my mental health. Tier 1 helped me to stand up for myself and to no longer allow people to treat me how they chose to. I have the power to set the standard for how I am to be treated. In doing this I was able to get closer with God. As a result of the CGCC Discipleship Model, I have grown incredibly. I am thankful for Dr. Moody's guidance; he is truly a blessing to me and my family.

-. *Zakiya S.*

For a long time I struggled with learning how to define myself as a person. Having an identity is something I've always wanted. One that I feel authentically suites me. As of recently, Dr. Moody's teachings on Tier 1 have led to me starting to define myself as a Tier 1 Man. A man who takes care of himself in order to better care for others (Tier 2).

-*Profit S.*

I remember lying on my bed as the tears rolled down my face and the only words I could muster up to say was Lord, Help me. I was tired of living like this. Tired of trying to make my husband do what I think he needed to do. I was tired of having arguments and angry outbursts. I was tired of being an enabler. I needed relief and I needed it fast. I was mentally drained, physically run down and completely exhausted. I was literally walking around in a fog. It was enough to make me lose the little bit of my mind I had left. There were times, I felt like the life was being choked out of me. Satan was so busy trying to rip my marriage apart and all I wanted to do was prevent that from happening. Sigh, in my head, I could hear Dr. Moody's voice telling me Tier 1. Stay in Tier 1! You are not in Tier 1. I guess you can figure out, I had a hard time doing "self". I was so use to thinking about what he was thinking or how he would respond to this or that. It wasn't easy for someone like me who lived life always trying to prevent the bottom from falling out from underneath them. As I prayed God showed me I needed to get out of my own way, so he could fix it. By letting go and letting God. I was able to live again. I could have peace by leaving the heavy stuff to the Lord and doing what I needed to do for myself. Each day it got easier to do "self". I was able to let go of the enabling qualities that I had picked up along the way and just left it *to the Almighty. I was able to breathe again. I was able to smile again and in those moments when I felt weak and began to worry. I prayed harder and God gave me peace and kept me from trying to control every situation. Tier 1 allowed me to have peace while living in the madness. I had to take care of "self" first in order to be good for anyone else. You can do it, Dr. Moody would say and he was right, I did. God is restoring my marriage and God is restoring me. Tier 1 saved my life!*   .

-LaFonda & Renold F.

ACKNOWLEDGMENTS

I would like to first give honor to my Lord and Savior Jesus Christ who is the head of my life; the author and finisher of my faith. I would like to thank and dedicate this work to the late Mother Dorothy Beatrice Moody, for her unselfish love and support throughout my life and the wonderful Christian example she provided for me and my family. I would like to thank my wife, Rev. Sharon E. Lee-Moody, for her love and support throughout this process. I would like to thank my many clients who allowed me to facilitate their wholeness from brokenness journey, utilizing the Tier 1 schematic whose focus is the spiritual dimension for self-discovery. This book is dedicated to individuals throughout the world in their quest for wholeness, happiness and purpose. It is my prayer that none should perish after having sought the spiritual dimension for new life empowerment.

TIER 1:
DISCOVERING SELF
"NEW WINE, OLD SKINS"

REVISED EDITION

TABLE OF CONTENTS

INTRODUCTION

The mission of the church is to make disciples of Jesus Christ. Local churches provide the most significant arena through which disciple-making occurs. Disciples are persons who do and act in certain ways; they are not persons who just say yes to something, then go their own way. In this case, we are talking about disciples of Jesus Christ, so these disciples will in some way do and act like Jesus.[1]

Disciples stumble and fail, but disciples experience forgiveness and love through the grace of Jesus Christ. As a result of their failures or struggles disciples become grounded and secure in their relationship to God. This is the foundational basis for Christianity's theology of Grace. Moreover, an additional component of the theology of grace is that God's demonstrated favor to humankind warrants a response. Christian Disciples are people who demonstrate their love of and response to Christ by loving one another, as they love themselves. In other words, Christ empowers us to love ourselves.

In Charting the Course: A Workbook on Christian Discipleship, John P. Gilbert posits that:

John Wesley believed that Christians journey on a path toward human perfection – the way of salvation. The path toward perfection is marked by various types of grace. Prevenient grace is given to all persons, and works in their lives before they encounter Christ. At some point, prevenient grace moves people to be convicted of their sins, a gift called convincing grace. When people are moved to repent of their sins, they receive justifying grace, assuring them of God's presence in their lives and giving them new life in Christ or Christian identity. Sanctifying grace moves people onward toward perfection. Such movement of grace reminds us that Wesley believed Christians are on a spiritual pilgrimage. For Wesley, the movement of grace upon grace is evidenced by continual growth in love of God and neighbor.[2]

This position of God's grace is vitally important, as it is the foundational truth that allows Christians to develop a healthy spiritual formation while journeying through the ups and downs of life. Many believers fall by the way side or through the cracks because when they are met with life's struggles, they lose faith and give up. Theologian John Gilbert states:

> In order to facilitate continual growth in persons seeking to grow deeper as disciples, Wesley organized the people called the Methodists into groups for public service. As people experienced God through those service encounters, they moved into trial bands. If they were growing as a result of their experiences in a trial band, they became members in a united society or church. Each person in the united society also belonged to a smaller group, called a class, which was located in the person's neighborhood. Some moved into bands, which were voluntary, smaller groups that met for confession, prayer, and spiritual growth. Through fellowship and Christian conversation, bands gained mutual accountability, nurture and growth in grace. Wesley's process allowed people to move through stages of growth and development toward spiritual maturity – always growing deeper in their love of God and neighbor. [3]

Tier 1 is a Spiritual Formation Model that is grounded in the development of the self. Tier 1 is a process that understands the importance of investing in the self for healthy spiritual formation. This breaks from sequences of the traditional J-O-Y (Jesus, Others, Self) Model which equates healthy spiritual formation in an infrastructure that places God first, others second, and self thirdly. Tier 1 departs from that model, and places the 'self' first, others second, and the global community thirdly. While I earnestly understand the sincere intentions of this model which places the needs of others before self, I believe that there is a biblical mandate for believers to be grounded in God and also grounded in a matured self (Tier 1) before they can effectively interface with others. Too many Christians live defeated lives, because there is no investment in the self. Many Christians prematurely enter ministry and attempt to pour into the lives of others while having a deficit in 'self' development. This is a recipe for disappointment and failure. Any effort to mask one's spiritual void by assisting others, is troubling. Tier 1 is a concept that empowers 'self' development and accepts God as the Core or Center of one's purpose for living. Healthy love of self is NOT the same as the narcissistic self-love prevalent in our culture today. Narcissism has its' roots in in our tainted and stained carnal nature. The Scriptures records:

(2Ti 3:1) This know also, that in the last days perilous times shall come.

(2Ti 3:2) For men shall be lovers of their own selves, covetous, boasters, proud, blasphemers, disobedient to parents, unthankful, unholy,

(2Ti 3:3) Without natural affection, trucebreakers, false accusers, incontinent, fierce, despisers of those that are good,
(2Ti 3:4) Traitors, heady, highminded, lovers of pleasures more than lovers of God;

(2Ti 3:5) Having a form of godliness, but denying the power thereof: from such turn away.

(2Ti 3:6) For of this sort are they which creep into houses, and lead captive silly women laden with sins, led away with divers lusts,

(2Ti 3:7) Ever learning, and never able to come to the knowledge of the truth.

(2Ti 3:8) Now as Jannes and Jambres withstood Moses, so do these also resist the truth: men of corrupt minds, reprobate concerning the faith.

(2Ti 3:9) But they shall proceed no further: for their folly shall be manifest unto all men, as theirs also was.

Narcissism is self-love that negates the encounter, experience and redemptive plan that God offers. The narcissists become their own god and establishes their own standards for living. To the contrary, love of self is a by-product of the believer's conversion, as we discover our identity, wholeness and purpose in Christ. I believe an investment in the development of the self is consistent with Scripture.

(Heb 5:12) For when for the time ye ought to be teachers, ye have need that one teach you again which be the first principles of the oracles of God; and are become such as have need of milk, and not of strong meat.

(Heb 5:13) For every one that useth milk is unskilful in the word of righteousness: for he is a babe.

(Heb 5:14) But strong meat belongeth to them that are of full age, even those who by reason of use have their senses exercised to discern both good and evil.

I believe new believers need to invest in a spiritual formation process that would allow them to develop into mature Christians. The Scriptures admonish the believers to, "Study to shew thyself approved unto God, a workman that needeth not to be ashamed, rightly dividing the word of truth. But shun profane and vain babblings: for they will increase unto more ungodliness." Healthy spiritual formation is accessed through exuberant worship and fostered through an intentional discipleship series. Healthy spiritual formation can circumvent the narcissistic influence of our culture. Believers today are exposed to the negative influences of secularism from the moment we are birthed.

I believe one cannot fully love another, if there is no healthy love of "self". Unfortunately, we are creatures of habit and resistant to change. There is no way we can fully embrace the 'new wine' of the Spirit in our 'old skins.' Jesus said, "Neither do men put new wine into old bottles: else the bottles break, and the wine runneth out, and the bottles perish: but they put new wine into new bottles, and both are preserved." This suggests we have to make adjustments to our old ways of thinking. Many Christians misunderstand Jesus' admonition to His disciples when He said "If any man will come after me, let him deny himself, and take up His cross, and follow me. For whosoever will save his life shall lose it; and whosoever will lose his life for my sake shall find it." (Matthew 16: 24-25). This denial of the "self" in this passage refers to one's carnal nature and lustful desires, not one's total person. It is tragic that many new believers attempt to extend Christian love to others, when there was no investment in the development of the self. I believe God does not want believers to self-sacrifice in this manner. That is not, "denying oneself and following Christ when prematurely enter ministry to others. That is naivety! The Apostle Paul prayed, "Brethren, my heart's desire to God for Israel is, that they might be saved. For I bear them record that they have a zeal of God, but not according to knowledge. For they being ignorant of God's righteousness, and going about to establish their own righteousness, have not submitted themselves unto the righteousness of God"[6]

Tier 1 is a Spiritual Formation Model that embraces the development of the self. This is a paradigm shift from the traditional view and provides a 'Social Theory of Change' around discipleship. I believe this investment in the self is paramount for living an effective and victorious Christian life. Healthy spiritual formation models focus on one disciple at a time. Every church will not be a mega-church. The magnitude and scope of the ministry is not diminished by the size of the membership roster.

Unfortunately, many churches have fed into the quantity of their congregations and not the quality of the message and the spiritual formation process. Believers are manufactured and pushed through an assembly line with no care to the quality of the end-product. Our narcissistic culture has bled into the fabric of our mission & vision statements and has caused us to stray away from the biblical mandate to 'go and make disciples of men.' One disciple at a time. A healthy believer should be secured in Worship (intimacy) and Discipleship (identity development) which is the focus of Tier 1.

Tier 2 is a normal progression the **other**. Tier 2 encompasses Fellowship (accountability) and Ministry (reciprocity). Finally, healthy spiritual formation will progress to Tier 3 for Evangelism. This involves missions and global marketplace issues. Collaboration with ecumenism and social community groups and issues. This safeguards one from Cultism.

ENDNOTES

[1]John P. Gilbert, Theresa Gilbert, Patty Johansen and Jay Regenniter, Charting the Course: A Workbook on Christian Discipleship (Philadelphia, PA: Fortress Press, 1986), 15.
[2]Gilbert, 40.
[3]Ibid. 45.
[4]Holy Bible, 2 Tim 2:15-16.
[5]Ibid. Matt 9:17b
[6]Ibid. Rom 10:1-3

CHAPTER ONE
WHO IS THE SELF?

There are many disciplines that shape the discussion of the self. Webster defines self as the entire person of an individual; the union of elements as body, emotions, thoughts, spirit and sensations that constitute the individuality and identity of a person. Therefore, the discussion of self has to do with identity. Psychologist understand the self through the lens of theories as Attachment Theory, Family Systems Theory, Freudian Theory of Personality, and B.F. Skinner's Theory of Operant Conditioning, to name a few. Rudi Dallos states that "Attachment Theory can be regarded as offering an important perspective on the development of self. This includes ideas about how the child develops an identity, an idea of who we they and how they came to be the way they are. This can be seen to fit with a social constructionist approach which emphasizes psychological theory and therapy as necessarily personal, subjective and concerned with the construction of meanings and identities. This theory understands attachment as a vital ingredient to psychosocial development. As an infant interacts with caregivers, they develop consciousness and identity through the level of care and attention given to the attachment. Touch, comfort, nurturing, cuddling, feeding, and holding shapes an infants' sense of identity, worth and well-being. The opposite is true. The lack of touch, comfort, nurturing and cuddling develops a poor sense of self, worth and well-being. The identity of the self that emerges progresses into the young child, teen, young adult and adult. Those early attachments serve to shape the psychosocial development of the infant and follows through to the adult. Of course maladjustments occur as the child matures, but the impact of those initial attachments are significant.

Dallos further posits, "When an adult comforts a child, their responses are synchronized with the child's needs. This can foster a feeling of contact, of being joined and experiencing the adult as part of oneself. The strengths and competencies of the adult are in this way incorporated into a sense of the self. Finally, it suggests that the child is also able to internalize or mirror the actions of the adult." This is the self that matures and eventually develops a quest for wholeness, purpose and understanding of life. This is the self that may come to faith and is initiated into the Body of Christ. Healthy spiritual formation must take into account the psychosocial state of individuals that encounter the spiritual dimension.

Any mystical discussion on who we are, how we came to be, and our purpose for living, must consider spirituality, which is a significant component of one's total person. However, we cannot start the discussion of spirituality by focusing on the self. Rick Warren, in his book entitled, Purpose Driven Life, states "You cannot arrive at your life's purpose by starting with a focus on yourself. You must begin with God, your Creator. You exist only because God wills that you exist. You were made by God and for God. It is only in God that we discover our origin, our identity, our purpose, our significance, and our destiny. Every other path leads to a dead end. The Scripture records:

> Jer 2:13 For my people have committed two evils; they have forsaken me the fountain of living waters, and hewed them out cisterns, broken cisterns, that can hold no water.

Our true self is our spiritual self; the person God created us to be. We discover our true selves when we take off the 'old skins' of how the world has shaped and defined us. **Spirituality is the highest expression of ourselves.** The Word of God says, "Therefore if any man be in Christ, he is a new creature: old things are passed away; behold, all things are become new." Believers discover new identity in Christ. Understanding identity in Christ requires understanding of the new birth process. Believers are "born-again." Believers are born of the Spirit. The new birth process begins the moment a person accepts Jesus as Lord and Savior. At that moment the individual is infused with the Holy Spirit. This "regeneration" is designed to recapture identity once had with God before the fall of humanity into sinful nature. In a discussion with His disciples, Jesus describes the spiritual renewal process in the following way:

(Mat 9:10) And it came to pass, as Jesus sat at meat in the house, behold, many publicans and sinners came and sat down with him and his disciples.

(Mat 9:11) And when the Pharisees saw it, they said unto his disciples, Why eateth your Master with publicans and sinners?

(Mat 9:12) But when Jesus heard that, he said unto them, They that be whole need not a physician, but they that are sick.

(Mat 9:16) No man putteth a piece of new cloth unto an old garment, for that which is put in to fill it up taketh from the garment, and the rent is made worse.

(Mat 9:17) Neither do men put new wine into old bottles: else the bottles break, and the wine runneth out, and the bottles perish: but they put new wine into new bottles, and both are preserved.

This passage of scripture reveals a significant fact around the new birth of believers. It suggests that believers have to remove the old skins (carnal self) in order to preserve the new wine (Holy Spirit). One's new identity is one's true self. Understandably, new birth is a process that requires intentionality. When attention to healthy spiritual formation is not achieved, believers experience spiritual distress or anxiety. Ronald Richardson describes this phenomena from a Family Systems Theory perspective. He posits, "At its most basic level, anxiety, is about the threat to the loss of who we are – our "self." At some preconscious, instinctual level, this is what the infant fears in the separation from the primary caregiver. Being so dependent, the infant needs that parent's presence in order to survive. Abandonment is the worst thing that could happen." I propose that there is a parallel truth apparent in Richardson's point that could be ascribed to the new birth process. New believers need to develop an intimate relationship with Jesus. New believers need their minds to be transformed through a methodical discipleship series. New believers need their hearts to be purified through the intimacy of sincere worship. In this way, new believers, like the infant, needs God's presence in order to survive. "As the deer panteth for the water, so my soul longeth after Thee." When the thief comes to kill, steal and destroy, he is attempting to rob the believer of his new identity and to isolate them to the point of feeling abandoned. Abandonment causes spiritual distress and anxiety. Intentional worship and discipleship allows the freshness of the Spirit to be poured into new wineskins. In this way, they both are preserved! Healthy spiritual formation invokes the presence of God in the lives of the believers. The Epistles are letters written to encourage believers and will aid to offset spiritual distress. The Apostle Paul records:

(2Co 4:6) For God, who commanded the light to shine out of darkness, hath shined in our hearts, to give the light of the knowledge of the glory of God in the face of Jesus Christ.

(2Co 4:7) But we have this treasure in earthen vessels, that the excellency of the power may be of God, and not of us.

(2Co 4:8) We are troubled on every side, yet not distressed; we are perplexed, but not in despair;

(2Co 4:9) Persecuted, but not forsaken; cast down, but not destroyed;

(2Co 4:10) Always bearing about in the body the dying of the Lord Jesus, that the life also of Jesus might be made manifest in our body.

(2Co 4:11) For we which live are always delivered unto death for Jesus' sake, that the life also of Jesus might be made manifest in our mortal flesh.

The presence of God is an important ingredient to the new and true self. In a discussion with the disciples before Jesus ascended, He promised them that He would always be present with them. Jesus said, "And I will pray the Father, and He shall give you another Comforter, that He may abide with you for ever; Even the Spirit of truth; whom the world cannot receive, because it seeth Him not, neither knoweth Him: but ye know Him; for He dwelleth with you, and shall be in you. I will not leave you comfortless: I will come to you." The indwelling presence of God is the highlight of the new birth process. The mere fact that the Creator comes and takes His abode (new wine) in the believer (old skins) is the greatest point of reference for one's new identity.

(Col 3:1) If ye then be risen with Christ, seek those things which are above, where Christ sitteth on the right hand of God.

(Col 3:2) Set your affection on things above, not on things on the earth.

(Col 3:3) For ye are dead, and <u>your life is hid with Christ in God</u>.

(Col 3:8) But now ye also put off all these; anger, wrath, malice, blasphemy, filthy communication out of your mouth.

(Col 3:9) Lie not one to another, seeing that ye have <u>put off the old man</u> with his deeds;

(Col 3:10) And have <u>put on the new man</u>, which is renewed in knowledge after the image of him that created him:

Rick Warren states, "Many people try to use God for their own self-actualization, but that is a reversal of nature and is doomed to failure. You were made for God, not vice-versa, and life is about letting God use you for His purposes, not using Him for your own purposes. It is about becoming what God created you to be." As we begin our spiritual journey, upon receiving the freshness of the Spirit, it is important to reconcile past psycho-social predispositions that may hinder healthy spiritual formation. In other words, we need to have resolved and/or be mindful of past trauma and idiosyncrasies that may have active triggers. We need to be aware of those predispositions that may interfere with healthy interpersonal group dynamics.

Richardson's Bowen Family Systems Theory examines how individuals differentiate within the emotional system of one's family of origin. This theory explores how our family's genome impact us. Specifically, it examines our parents and sibling placement. Being the older child or the middle child or the younger child, impacts emotional development. This perspective is important because our family of origin shapes the way we interact with others in the greater community. Why is this germane to my discussion of self? Because family orientation influence integration into the Body of Christ. The manner in which one navigates and thrives in their family of origin, is how they present in fellowship with believers. Often-time when we see contentious group dynamics and strife, its stems from carnal interpersonal development.

(Jas 4:1) From whence come wars and fightings among you? come they not hence, even of your lusts that war in your members?

(Jas 4:2) Ye lust, and have not: ye kill, and desire to have, and cannot obtain: ye fight and war, yet ye have not, because ye ask not.

(Jas 4:3) Ye ask, and receive not, because ye ask amiss, that ye may consume it upon your lusts.

(Jas 4:4) Ye adulterers and adulteresses, know ye not that the friendship of the world is enmity with God? whosoever therefore will be a friend of the world is the enemy of God.

(Jas 4:5) Do ye think that the scripture saith in vain, The spirit that dwelleth in us lusteth to envy?

(Jas 4:6) But he giveth more grace. Wherefore he saith, God resisteth the proud, but giveth grace unto the humble.

(Jas 4:7) Submit yourselves therefore to God. Resist the devil, and he will flee from you.

(Jas 4:8) Draw nigh to God, and he will draw nigh to you. Cleanse *your* hands, ye sinners; and purify *your* hearts, *ye* double minded.

Unfortunately, many of these mannerisms are carnal and self-serving. These old skins are what we bring into our new birth experience. We can't simply try to worship over or suppress these experiences. They have a way of keep re-surfacing. Richardson states, "The family we grew up in, is the first, most powerful, longest lasting, and nearly indelible training we get for how to be a part of a group and to function within it. When the level of anxiety goes up and we become anxious, we tend to revert to our old family patterns and ways of functioning."[9]

We have to consciously submit these orientations to God, so God can transform us through His Word. In this way we could be authentic to who we are, and to who we are becoming. Instability occurs when who we think ourselves to be, is different from how we are behaving.

The gap between the two is cognitive dissonance. The power of the 'new wine' is that it creates in us a new heart and renews in in us a right spirit. It serves to bridge that gap. The Scriptures say that "we are predestined to be conformed to the image of the Son (Jesus)." As the indwelling presence of God (new wine) comforts the believer and synchronizes with their needs, the believer becomes one with the Spirit. Not only do we, internalize this comfort, but we mirror this phenomena. We are transformed into the very image of God as we encounter God. We are in fact being born again. Wow!

(2Co 3:17) Now the Lord is that Spirit: and where the Spirit of the Lord is, there is liberty.

(2Co 3:18) But we all, with open face beholding as in a glass the glory of the Lord, are changed into the same image from glory to glory, even as by the Spirit of the Lord.

Healthy spiritual formation is fostered through Worship, Discipleship, Ministry, Fellowship and Evangelism. This will be discussed in later chapters. Healthy spiritual formation of the self, the born-again self is all about discovering the new identity that we have in Christ. Tier 1 focuses on Worship and Discipleship. Spiritual formation and discovery of the self, our true self in Christ, is supported by the help of spiritual directors. Spiritual directors can be mentors, pastors, elders, family and friends who will come along side you and assist the Holy Spirit in aiding you discover the new you. Howard Stone states, "Spiritual direction is not a mystical process requiring arcane knowledge of esoteric spiritual formation. The director does, however, need experience and maturity in life. These qualities do not relate to chronological age of academic degrees. Rather, you must be able to sustain relationships and to listen, and you must be a person of prayer. While spiritual life can be confusing and enigmatic, the director may take comfort in knowing that common sense is the most reliable guide, when coupled with an attitude of acute awareness and openness to others' experiences and meanings."[11]

To this end, spiritual directors play a vital role in assisting the believer in discovering self. Stone was very clear to mark the difference between directors and therapist. "Therapist strive to resolve people's problems, or at least to help them respond to difficulties in a healthier way, whereas spiritual director's focus on helping people discern God's hand in their lives, to engage in a dialogue with God, and to determine the most appropriate response to God's action. Simply put, spiritual directors offer assistance to persons in their growing relationship with God." I strongly believe, that many new believers never mature into healthy believers because they did not embrace the spiritual direction given by guides sent from God to assist them. Discovering self is a meticulous process. The art of pouring new wine into old skins is the wonderful work of the new birth experience and requires intentional disciplines to accomplish the desired end, which is a healthy mature believer enveloped in a new identity in Christ.

Lifelong learning is the key to spiritual growth. Spiritual well-being is a by-product of spiritual growth. In other words, we learn that self-care is vitally important to longevity. Dr. Hallas, a family practice physician, sates, "Although research shows that religious commitment and activity have a positive impact on health, research done on ordained ministers from various churches and on rostered lay leaders identifies significant health problems that need to be addressed. These problems include: Stress and depression; Weight and lack of physical activity; Nutrition and cholesterol; and High blood pressure and heart disease." I found this very profound. We normally expect the ministers and lay leaders to be the healthiest in the community of faith. Ministers and lay leaders are those who are providing spiritual direction to others and assisting new believers in discovering self. One would think that the ministers and the lay leaders would be the examples of healthy spiritual being. This is why it is so important to do Tier 1 work. Tier 1 is all about self. We need to be grounded in self-care and preservation. This is why Jesus said, "but they put new wine into new bottles, and both are preserved." The freshness of the Spirit is preserved in a new framework (mentally, physically, spiritually, and emotionally). Preservation is a sign of healthy spiritual formation. *Tier 1 is all about preserving self.*

As we discover self, as God created us to be, then we are able to understand and fulfill our purpose. Understanding purpose provides wholeness, guides direction, empowers will, informs clarity, sustains effort and offsets depression and anxiety. When believers discover self and incorporate disciplines to sustain and preserve self, then they are ready for Tier 2 (other) and Tier 3 (global community). The problem for many believers is that they enter the ministry (Tier 2) and the marketplace (Tier 3) without having invested in self (Tier 1). I will discuss this more in later chapters and Tier 2 and 3 in subsequent volumes. Discovering self is important because it filters the forces of good and evil in the world and how it influences our thoughts, attitudes, and behavior. Greenleaf concludes that, "What happens to our values, and therefore to the quality of our civilization in the future, will be shaped by the conceptions of individuals that are born of inspiration." Discovering self, and assisting others in discovering self is vitally important to the perpetuation of our great legacy, with all of its values, mores and traditions.

(Heb 12:1) Wherefore seeing we also are compassed about with so great a cloud of witnesses, let us lay aside every weight, and the sin which doth so easily beset us, and let us run with patience the race that is set before us,

(Heb 12:2) Looking unto Jesus the author and finisher of our faith; who for the joy that was set before him endured the cross, despising the shame, and is set down at the right hand of the throne of God.

(Heb 12:3) For consider him that endured such contradiction of sinners against himself, lest ye be wearied and faint in your minds.

ENDNOTES

[1]Dallos, 12.
[2]Dallos, 33.
[3]Warren, Purpose Driven Life, 18.
[4]Holy Bible, 2 Cor 5:17
[5]Richardson, Creating a Healthier Church, 48-49.
[6]Holy Bible, Ps 42:1
[7]Ibid. John 14:16-18.
[8]Warren, Purpose Driven Life, 18-19.
[9]Ibid. ix.
[10]Holy Bible, Ro 8:29.
[11]Stone, 125.
[12]Ibid, 125,6.
[13]Halaas. 1,2
[14]Holy Bible, Matt 9:17b
[15]Greenleaf, 8.

CHAPTER TWO

BIBLICAL MANDATE AND THE CONTEMPORARY CHURCH

I believe many Christians are defeated today because the contemporary church has failed to maintain key factors of discipleship in our spiritual formation models. John Wesley once stated:

> Healthy discipleship-formation processes require various entry points into the process, since persons may enter the disciple-formation process at various points on their faith journey. Healthy discipleship-formation processes focus on the faith journey of individuals and the congregation. They focus on lifelong formation, rather than on programs that provide quick fixes.[1]

I strongly believe many Christians fail because the Gospel message has been compromised and commercialized in a narcissistic culture which has no patience and only focuses on the present. We have become a microwave society and church. Churches have turned their attention to wanting bigger, larger and mega. This preoccupation with the multitude and not the 'individual' has caused many to be relegated to the sidelines. "Practices of faith, means of grace, and the church-owned definition of disciple will become the developing guidelines for what it means to grow in faith"[2]

Rick Warren posits in his book, *The Purpose Driven Church: Growth Without Compromising Your Message & Mission*:

> I've found it interesting to observe that most of the parachurch movements begun in the past forty years tend to specialize in one of the purposes (Worship, Ministry, Discipleship, Fellowship, and Evangelism) of the church. From time to time God has raised up a parachurch movement to reemphasize a neglected purpose of the church. I believe it is valid, and even helpful to the church,

for parachurch organizations to focus on a single purpose. It allows their emphasis to have greater impact on the church.[3]

I believe Christianity is important! It serves as a viable resource to navigate people through the vicissitudes of life. Christianity matters because it offers a blueprint that explores the spiritual dimension and answers humanity's innermost quest for wholeness, purpose and happiness.

With an increased incidence of defeated and unfulfilled Christians being recognized and reported in data from Christian researchers, the need for a healthy Spiritual Formation Model has become apparent. A new Pew Research Center Survey records, "We've known for some time that the number of Americans who say they have no religion has been growing. But while this group does not identify with a specific religious tradition or denomination, the "nones" are not uniformly against religion having a role in society." The Pew Research Center also reports the following data:

We asked all respondents whether religion is gaining or losing influence in American life, and 72% of U.S. adults (including 70% of the religiously unaffiliated) said religion is losing influence. We then asked whether this is a good thing or a bad thing, and, not surprisingly, "nones" were much more likely than other major religious groups to say that the declining influence of religion in American life is a good thing. The results, however, were not completely one-sided. In fact, religiously unaffiliated people who perceive religion's influence as declining was split on whether this is a good thing or a bad thing. About a third of "nones" overall (34%) said it is good that religion is losing influence, while a similar share (30%) said this is bad. "Nones" include atheists and agnostics as well as people who have no religion in particular. Among only atheists and agnostics, half (50%) see religion's influence as declining and see this as a good thing, while only 12% say it's a bad thing. But among those who say their religion is "nothing in particular," 37% say religion's declining influence is a bad thing and 27% say it's a good thing.[6]

The report also states:

> We found in 2012 that 14% of "nones" said religion is very important in their lives, and another 19% said it is somewhat important. About two-thirds of the unaffiliated (68%) believe in God – 30% said they're "absolutely certain" about God's existence – and 21% reported praying daily. Only one-in-ten people whose religion is "nothing in particular" said they are looking for a religion that is right for them, but there appears to be a significant subset of Americans who are comfortable with religion having a role in their life even without having an official religious affiliation.[7]

Mark Shaw posits, "I maintain that the evangelical church is weak, self-indulgent, and superficial. While evangelical churches are filling up with spectators, they are emptying out of disciples. I propose the solution to be the obedience to Christ's commission to 'make disciples,' to teach Christians to obey everything Christ commanded." I believe a commercialized and compromised gospel within a culture of narcissism, materialism and apathy provides an unhealthy congregational context for respondents to achieve the victorious Christian life offered freely by God. "While mainline Protestant denominations hemorrhaged members during the 1970's – the largest Presbyterian, Episcopal, and Methodist denominations all lost at least 10 percent of their members between 1965 and 1975 – many suburban evangelical churches began the rapid growth that would make them the megachurches of subsequent decades." The Spiritual Formations Movement embraced the importance of the disciple-formation process. Notwithstanding, the turn of the 21st Century, was met with more incidences and prevalence of defeated Christians being reported. There is a need for a clear and concise Spiritual Formation Model that is consistent with foundational truths and the realities of the Christian journey.

Churches are **mandated** to create an atmosphere that allows every congregant to live an effective Christian life. 'The Great Commandment' says:

[handwritten: axis 1] And thou shall love the Lord with all thy heart, and with all thy soul, and with thy entire mind, and with all thy strength: this is the first commandment. And the second is like, namely *[handwritten: axis 4]* this, thou shall love thy neighbor as thyself. There is none other commandment greater than these. (St. Mark 12: 30 & 31).

'The Great Commission' says:

[handwritten: Tier 3] Go ye therefore, and teach all nations baptizing them in the name of the Father, and of the Son, and of the Holy Ghost; Teaching them to observe all things whatsoever I have *[handwritten: Discipl Ship]* commanded you: and, lo, I am with you always, even unto the end of the world (St. Matthew 28: 19 & 20).

'The Great Commission' and 'The Great Commandment' provide a theological foundation profitable for "doctrine, for reproof, for correction, for instruction in righteousness; that the man/woman of God may be perfect, thoroughly furnished unto all good works." (II Timothy 3: 16b – 17).

'The Great Commandment' and 'The Great Commission' generate a five-fold approach for healthy spiritual formation. Those factors are indispensable to the process. They are: Worship, Discipleship, Ministry, Fellowship, and Evangelism. I believe that a Spiritual Formation Model that employs these five factors would bridge the gap of those who have failed, fallen or fell away from the Faith. I believe these factors are indispensable for effective Christian living. These five factors were accompanied by five movements of the church worldwide. They were the **Worship Renewal Movement**,

the Spiritual Formations Movement, the Small Group/ Pastoral Care Movement, the Lay Renewal Movement and the Church Growth Movement, respectively.

ENDNOTES

[1]Gilbert, 93.

[2]Gilbert, 93.

[3]Warren, The Purpose Driven Church, 126.

[4]Ronald Richardson, Creating a Healthier Church (Minneapolis: Fortress Press, 1996), 25.

[5]Pew Research Center, "Is Religion's Declining Influence Good or Bad? Those without Religious Affiliation are Divided," accessed September 23, 2014, http://www.pewresearch.org/fact-tank/2014/09/23/is-religions- declining-influence-good-or-bad-those-without-religious-affiliation-are-divided.

[6] Ibid.

[7]Ibid.

[8]Mark Shaw, 10 Great Ideas from Church History: A Decision-Makers Guide to Shaping Your Church (Downers Grove, Illinois: InterVarsity Press, 1997), 135.

[9]JohnTurner, Bill Bright & Campus Crusade for Christ: The Renewal of Evangelicalism in Postwar America (Chapel Hill: The University of North Carolina Press, 2008), 147.

CHAPTER THREE

DEVELOPING A HEALTHY SPIRITUAL FORMATION MODEL

I employed the following methodology as part of the preparation to satisfy the requirements to obtain the Doctorate of Ministry Degree from Drew University, which I successfully completed in May 2015.

Phase One: The overall goal of this project was to develop a Spiritual Formation Model to be implemented at the Chosen Generation Community Church in Plainfield, New Jersey.

> Plainfield is nicknamed "The Queen City". It was settled in 1684 by Quakers, and incorporated as city in 1869. A short train ride from New York City, Plainfield is a bedroom suburb in the New York metropolitan area; it has become the urban center of 10 closely allied municipalities, with diversified industries, including printing and the manufacture of chemicals, clothing, electronic equipment, and vehicular parts.[1]

Plainfield has a population of 50, 244 residents; 25,280 males (50.3%) and 24,964 females (49.7%). The median age is 33.3. The median income is $50,076. 44% are married; 71% speak English; 25% speak Spanish. 21% are Caucasian; 61% are African-American; 5% are mixed race; and 11% are other.[2]

Plainfield is comprised of many small businesses; one high school; several middle schools and elementary schools. There are over 125 churches in Plainfield. Plainfield is comprised of faith-based institutions, service providers, small businesses and for-profit corporations, who could benefit from favorable outcomes of project indicators which may impact the social theory of change in Plainfield. Like many townships, Plainfield has social issues that negatively impact its' citizenry.

The purpose for this project was multi-faceted. I wanted to investigate and analyze available information on areas of Christian development so that I could isolate and understand those factors that seemed critical for turning new converts into well-grounded disciples. Review of the Literature: The information from the investigation of several spiritual formation models were analyzed in order to determine what common factors they possessed. These factors were then designated "indispensable factors." These factors were compared to those factors that surfaced as a result of my project survey. I used the findings from the data analysis of this project to create an actual model.

I selected four urban Northern New Jersey churches for the project. The selected churches were assigned a letter (A,B,C, & D) to be used in lieu of the church name in an effort to protect and safeguard the privacy of the church and its' congregants. The project surveyed the adult population of the current membership rosters of the four diverse churches selected: 1. Church A, Plainfield, NJ; 2. Church B, Newark, NJ; 3. Church C, Newark, NJ; and 4. Church D, East Orange, NJ. The survey involved 80 adult men and women. The scope of this survey was limited to these four (4) Northern New Jersey urban churches with predominantly African-American memberships. Consequently inferences will be limited to churches with similar demographics and cultural attributes.

Phase Two: Once indispensable factors were identified I created an anonymous, empirical, objective self-report survey that would be given to selected churches membership for the purposes of understanding the call to discipleship and the five indispensable factors or hereafter referred as the "chief paradigm." The goal of the survey was to determine if respondents were familiar with those five indispensable factors and its' impact on their spiritual formation. Special attention was given to the respondents understanding of the spiritual formation processes offered at the selected churches and their ability to equip them for spiritual maturity. I also examined the path to discipleship from the initial "call to discipleship" through the spiritual formation process that selected churches employed. The survey further attempted to examine the respondents' knowledge of the selected churches Mission Statement and the churches ability to abide by them.

Self-Report validation has been well documented in the literature. The reliability and validity of Self-Report studies have received much attention by research practitioners. Research by P.J. Frawley tested the reliability and validity of the quantitative inventory and the veracity of self-reporting. "The primary intention was to demonstrate the reliability and validity of self-reporting as a diagnostic tool. The results from the investigation supported the hypothesis that individuals can produce valid responses to self-report questionnaires.[3]

PAC chose to use a Self-Report Survey for this project because PAC wanted a firsthand account from members of the four selected churches on the current state of affairs surrounding discipleship in their local church. Often, the leadership is oblivious to the quality of work they are doing. Most church leaders either believe that they are doing fine or don't care. Many local churches don't have a quality assurance measure or an evaluative diagnostic tool in place to solicit feedback from the membership. Self-Report Surveys have demonstrated effectiveness as a viable and reliable diagnostic tool to collect data from people, so for that purpose it was employed for this project. PAC also elected for the survey to be anonymous so that respondents would feel free to express their true feelings without fear of negative repercussions.

Phase Three: I met with the ministry leadership from the four selected churches and introduced the DMIN project goals, objectives, scope and processes. From these four selected churches I created the Project Advisory Committee (PAC) consistent with DMIN guidelines, which included a chairperson. PAC re-visited the initial survey created for feedback and feasibility for the targeted population. A revised DMIN survey was created. PAC identified the mechanism to disseminate and collect the Self-Report Surveys.

Phase Four: PAC distributed and collected the Self-Report Surveys over a three week period to the four selected churches for this project. The quantitative and qualitative data from the Self-Report (Appendix) Survey would be analyzed and used to create a Spiritual

Formation Model (Chapter IV) to be implemented at the Chosen Generation Community Church, Plainfield, New Jersey. This data will also be shared with selected churches for their edification and use. PAC met for a total of six sessions from November 2013 through April 2014. A Site Review was conducted on April 24, 2014 where PAC met with faculty advisor from Drew University.

Phase Five: Tier 1 of the Spiritual Formation Model would be implemented at the Chosen Generation Community Corporation. Tier 1 would be strategically integrated into therapeutic milieu for respondents in search of wholeness, purpose, reconciliation, mediation and spiritual direction. Eventually, there would be the natural progression to Tier 2 (other) and Tier 3 (global community/ marketplace).

ENDNOTES

[1]City of Plainfield Website, accessed 22 October 2014, www.Plainfield.com.

[2]City of Plainfield Website, accessed 22 October 2014, www.Plainfield.com.

[3]PJ Frawley, "The Validity of Self-Report Data," *Journal of Alcohol,* 49, no.5 (1988): 263-92.

CHAPTER FOUR
TIER 1 - CGGC
SPIRITUAL FORMATION
MODEL

Motto: *"Empowerment through Engagement"*

CHOSEN GENERATION
COMMUNITY
CHURCH
"NEW WINE, OLD SKINS"

THE MODEL OVERVIEW (3 COMPONENTS)

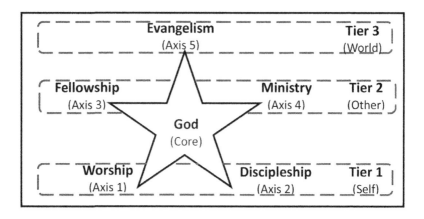

- THESE 5 FACTORS CAN BE QUANTIFIED TO PROVIDE EMPIRICAL DATA TO MINISTRIES

*Gathered data was analyzed used to create a Spiritual Formation Model to be used at Chosen Generation Community Church. The model comprises three (3) components: one (1) Core (God); five (5) indispensable factors (Worship, Discipleship, Fellowship, Ministry, and Evangelism); and three (3) Tiers (Self, Other, and World).

SPIRITUAL FORMATION MODEL OVERVIEW

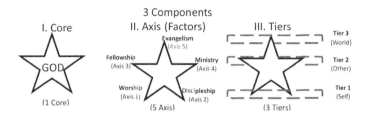

The **Core** of the CGCC Spiritual Formation Model is God. The Spiritual Formation Model provides a thorough examination of the Core attributes of God: Creator, Eternal Spirit, Trinity, Immutable, Omnipresent, Omnipotent, Omniscient, Covenant, and Sovereign. "God is a Spirit and those who worship Him must worship Him in Spirit and in Truth." (St. John 4:24) Recognition of the importance of the spiritual dimension in human development is vital. Spirituality is not a measure of a person's religion; it is the belief in a "higher power."

The Higher Power is one of the most amazing facts in human existence. This tremendous inflow of power is of such force that in its inrush it drives everything before it, casting out fear, hate, sickness, weakness, moral defeat, scattering them as though they had never touched you, refreshing and re-strengthening your life with health, happiness and goodness. Healthy Spiritual Formation is grounded in the existence of God. The Word of God says if anyone, "Believes in his heart, and confess with his mouth, that Jesus is Lord, he/she shall be saved." This confession commences new birth and initiates the process of salvation. The rejection of God (new wine) due to pride and arrogance is met with further demise. When we refuse to acknowledge God and worship Him, the consequences are not favorable.

(Jer 13:9) Thus saith the LORD, After this manner will I mar the pride of Judah, and the great pride of Jerusalem.

(Jer 13:10) This evil people, which refuse to hear my words, which walk in the imagination of their heart, and walk after other gods, to serve them, and to worship them, shall even be as this girdle, which is good for nothing.

(Jer 13:11) For as the girdle cleaveth to the loins of a man, so have I caused to cleave unto me the whole house of Israel and the whole house of Judah, saith the LORD; that they might be unto me for a people, and for a name, and for a praise, and for a glory: but they would not hear.

(Jer 13:12) Therefore thou shalt speak unto them this word; Thus saith the LORD God of Israel, **Every wineskin shall be filled with wine**: and they shall say unto thee, Do we not certainly know that every **wineskin shall be filled with wine**?

(Jer 13:13) Then shalt thou say unto them, Thus saith the LORD, Behold, I will fill all the inhabitants of this land, even the kings that sit upon David's throne, and the priests, and the prophets, and all the inhabitants of Jerusalem, with drunkenness.

(Jer 13:14) And I will dash them one against another, even the fathers and the sons together, saith the LORD: I will not pity, nor spare, nor have mercy, but destroy them.

(Jer 13:15) Hear ye, and give ear; be not proud: for the LORD hath spoken.

The **Axis** of the CGCC Spiritual Formation Model consists of the five (5) Indispensable Factors (Worship, Discipleship, Fellowship, Ministry, and Evangelism). These five factors correlate to five church movements that highlighted their importance.

The Tiers of the CGCC Spiritual Formation Model comprises of three (3) levels: Self, Other, and World

The Tiers of the CGCC Spiritual Formation Model comprises of three (3) levels: Self, Other, and World.

a.**Tier 1 (Self)**: Healthy Spiritual Formation is <u>accessed</u> and <u>fostered</u> through 'self' development by Spiritual Disciplines (Worship) and Foundational Truths (Discipleship).

b.**Tier 2 (Other)**: Healthy Spiritual Formation is <u>reinforced</u> (Fellowship) and demonstrated (Ministry) as a natural progression to the 'other' within a loving and affirming community.

c.**Tier 3 (World)**: Healthy Spiritual Formation is <u>fulfilled</u> as it extends to the 'world' (Evangelism) for Global impact and marketplace transformation to offset isolationism, cultism and narrow-mindedness.

Tier 1 examines the placement of the self within the larger framework of healthy spiritual formation. Being grounded in self means an individual understands God as core and through worship and discipleship become centered and aligned with purpose. Alignment produces the fruit of the spirit: love, joy, peace, longsuffering, gentleness, goodness, faith, temperance, and meekness. Spiritual formation is initiated through new birth. "If any man be in Christ Jesus, he is a new creation; Old things are passed away and behold all things become new." Born-again believers are likened to those receiving the 'new wine' of the Spirit.[4]

(Mat 9:16) No man putteth a piece of new cloth unto an old garment, for that which is put in to fill it up taketh from the garment, and the rent is made worse.

(Mat 9:17) Neither do men put new wine into old bottles: else the bottles break, and the wine runneth out, and the bottles perish: but they put new wine into new bottles, and both are preserved.

New wine cannot be put into old wineskins. The freshness of a regenerated spirit cannot reach its' fulfillment in the infrastructure of old fallen nature. New wine and old skins won't work. The spirit man has been renewed, but there remains the need to bring the soulish nature in alignment with the spirit. Many believers experience defeat in their lives because emotionally and mentally they are not equipped to accommodate the newness of the Spirit. Many psychosocial predispositions impede one's ability to embrace the newness of the Spirit. New wine, old skins. King David asked the Lord to "Create in me a clean heart, and re-new the right spirit within me." King David realized that his spiritual intentions were hampered by his old degenerate heart and soulish nature.

For this dilemma, Worship is the medium needed for heart-transformation. After the process of new birth, believers embrace intimacy with God through the worship experience. Worship is a matter of the heart. Through intimate worship with God, a believers' heart is re-shaped and moved toward God. Ezekiel recorded that, "God would take away that stony heart, and give us a heart of flesh." A heart of flesh is a softer heart that is open to the flow of the Spirit and empowers the believer to be sensitive to the pulse and heartbeat of the Spirit. It also empowers believers to be sensitive to their inner voice. It is in this phenomena where healing and restoration occurs. Believers become reconciled to God and one's true self. The re-created self is positioned and aligned with the Creator. Tier 1 (Self) is grounded in God (Core) and accessed through Worship. Read chapter 5 for the history of the Worship Movement.

Believer's healthy spiritual formation is fostered through an intentional **Discipleship** process. The new wine of the Spirit cannot find its' fulfillment in a degenerate mind; the result of the fallen nature. The Word of God admonishes believers to "Be not conformed to this world, but transformed by the renewing of your minds. That you may prove what is the acceptable will of God." Many believers cannot embrace the newness of the Spirit because mentally they are incapable of understanding or receiving biblical truths. The Word says we are born in sin and shaped in iniquity. We are therefore, naughty by nature. Our minds are corrupt and cannot receive the things of God. Rejection of the new wine of the Holy Spirit due to pride and arrogance will only further ensnare believers into a world-wind of calamity. "Pride always goes before destruction."[8]

The onset of the new birth or conversion ushers us into spiritual warfare, because the enemy of our souls refuses to let us walk in the freedom of the Spirit. So as a result we are in a struggle between the desires of the flesh (carnal nature) and the Spirit (new nature). The Bible says, "That the righteousness of the law might be fulfilled in us, who walk not after the flesh, but after the Spirit. For they that are after the flesh do mind the things of the flesh; but they that are after the Spirit the things of the Spirit. For to be carnally minded is death; but to be spiritually minded is life and peace. Because the carnal mind is enmity against God: for it is not subject to the law of God, neither indeed can be. So then they that are in the flesh cannot please God. But ye are not in the flesh, but in the Spirit, if so be that the Spirit of God dwell in you. Now if any man have not the Spirit of Christ, he is none of his." Scripture is clear. The flesh and the Spirit are mutually exclusive and cannot co-exist. The need for discipleship is apparent.

(Gal 5:16) This I say then, Walk in the Spirit, and ye shall not fulfil the lust of the flesh.

(Gal 5:17) For the flesh lusteth against the Spirit, and the Spirit against the flesh: and these are contrary the one to the other: so that ye cannot do the things that ye would.

Healthy Spiritual Formation is fostered through intentional Discipleship. The Word says: "Let this mind be in you, which was in Christ Jesus." The Word of God provides a framework for the believer to understand spiritual warfare: "For though we walk in the flesh, we do not war after the flesh: (For the weapons of our warfare are not carnal, but mighty through God to the pulling down of strong holds); Casting down imaginations, and every high thing that exalteth itself against the knowledge of God, and bringing into captivity every thought to the obedience of Christ;" Read Chapter 6 for the history of the Discipleship Movement.

Tier 1 (Self) is grounded in God (Core), accessed through Worship and fostered through Discipleship. The Tier 1 (Self) person is a spiritually grounded believer who has been regenerated in spirit. This is not an instantaneous affair but an ongoing process. Tier 1 is that wonderful place that King David referred to as "that secret place of the Most High." Healthy spiritual formation warns eliminates ill-prepared believers from entering into ministry. Tier 1 is a rallying point of reference when believers lose their footing and are about to fall into spiritual distress. Its' that secret place that allows you to recapture your purpose for living. Tier 1 is a vital resource and precious gem for believers living in a complex world of intense spiritual warfare.

> (Col 1:21)   And you, that were sometime alienated and enemies in your mind by wicked works, yet now hath he reconciled
>
> (Col 1:22)   In the body of his flesh through death, to present you holy and unblameable and unreproveable in his sight.

Tier 1 should be in every believers' toolbox!

ENDNOTES

[1]Holy Bible, Romans 9:10
[2] Ibid. Gal 5:22
[3]Ibid. I Corinthians 5:17
[4]Ibid. Matthew 9:16&17
[5]Ibid. Psalm 51:10
[6]Ibid. Ezekiel 11:9
[7]Ibid. Rom 12:1&2
[8]Ibid. Prov 16:18
[9]Ibid. Rom 8:4-9
[10]Ibid. Phil 2:5
[11]Ibid. 2 Cor10:3-6
[12]Ibid. Psalm 91:1

CHAPTER FIVE
WORSHIP RENEWAL MOVEMENT (WORSHIP)

The Renewal Movement was a major para church movement and refocused the importance of worship and how we worship. It began with the Jesus Movement in the early 1970s and was followed by the Charismatic and Liturgical renewals. Most recently, the contemporary worship emphasis has brought us new music, new worship forms, and a greater emphasis on corporate worship. Music styles like those created by Christian music producers like Maranatha, Hosanna and Integrity have played a major role in shaping how worship styles have changed and multiplied in recent years.[1]

Worship has always been a vital part of the life in the church. Worship is a reverence rendered unto God; a form of religious practice with its creed and ritual. Worship is both individual and corporate. Nathan Smith cites George Malone's description of a vision of worship which he found in a Sunday bulletin of a church that was experiencing renewal.

> We believe worship of God should be spiritual. Therefore: We remain flexible and yielded to the leading of the Spirit to direct our worship. We believe worship of God should be inspirational. Therefore: We give a great place to music in our worship. We believe worship of God should be intelligent. Therefore: Our services are designed with great emphasis upon teaching the Word of God that He might instruct how He should be worshiped. We believe worship of God should be sacramental. Therefore: We give ourselves to weekly observance of the Lord's Supper. We believe worship of God is fruitful. Therefore: We look to His love in our lives as the supreme manifestation that we have truly been worshiping Him.[2]

Corporate worship has evolved over the years and has been impacted by the renewal movements. As we examine the origins of corporate Christian worship Gordon Wakefield states, "One problem with regard to the origins of Christian worship, as Paul Bradshaw has shown, is that because accounts of it derive from later periods, there is little certainty as to what precisely Jewish worship was like at the time of Christ." To this end, there have been several renewal movements throughout the Christian history seeking out new meanings on the importance and expression of worship. All the renewal movements share a common idea – worship, both individual and corporate, are vitally important in the life of a Christian believer.

The twentieth century began with Liturgical Movement. Wakefield states, "The cornerstone of the liturgical movement is the reaffirmation of the Eucharist as the central act of Christian worship. It is the source of the Church's life, from which all prayer, devotion, witness and evangelization flows." To this end, the liturgical movement placed emphasis on the importance of the liturgy. Attention to the order of service had to be intentional, intelligent and meaningful. This requirement underscored the evolution of the renewal movements as the meaning, expression, rituals, and traditions around worship were sought. Wakefield states, "The liturgical movement insists that it is a service of Word and Sacrament, but with short lections and sermons the Word may not occupy much time." Certainly, this perspective is not the same among other traditions of faith. Methodism placed more importance on the delivery of the Word and Pentecostalism has revolutionized the preaching moment as the highlight of the service. I will not argue the merits of each view here but will agree that the Liturgical Movement impacted worship in important ways.

In the 1960's the Charismatic Renewal Movement emerged. Tom Smail states, "Because charismatic renewal is about our relationship to God, the renewal of our worship of God is one of its primary concern, and in fact over the last twenty-five years it has had a transforming effect on the worship of the churches." This vibrant period of renewal transcended denominational and liturgical traditions and ushered in an era of freedom and joy of the Holy Spirit. Smail further states:

> At the centre of that worship has been a new release of praise with its own distinctive characteristics that have supplemented and complemented the cherished treasury of

worship that the churches have inherited from the past. In this connection, it is not accident that the distinctive feature of charismatic worship, which has made a positive impression on most people who have come into contact with it, has been the corporate and spontaneous singing in tongues that has often been called 'singing in the Spirit.' That seems to me be the quintessence of worship in its charismatic mode, it gives expression to the distinctive features that inform the other parts of renewal worship and that characterize it as charismatic.[7]

While the theology of the charismatic movement is not accepted in varying Christian denominations, the importance and the impact of it on the subject of worship is invaluable.

For some Catholics in St. Charles County, the way to spiritual health is an outward expression of worship. Catholic Charismatic Renewal, as 25 year-old movement, has been sanctioned by several popes and many Catholic bishops. Most Catholic pastors are frightened of the Charismatic Renewal. Part of the reason is that they've seen people get into it and go on to leave the church.[8]

Notwithstanding, the belief that God communicates with His people is fundamental to Christian living and is an indispensable factor for living victoriously.

The expression of worship is intertwined with one's understanding of the meaning of worship. Graham Hughes explores the 'meaning of worship' in his book, Worship as Meaning, and poses many interesting questions around how the liturgy has evolved through the years. This information is important because it reveals that the meaning of worship has changed from one generation to the next. He states:

In the degree of generalization with which I am working, one may say that mainline Protestantism endeavors to make sense of God by reflecting from within its condition in modernity in order to say how and where God may be understood as fitting into this. Said again, protestant theology assumes the modern condition as given and is then faced with the task – self elucidatory and apologetic – of explaining God's place and function in this.[9]

This point is important in worship because it makes the worship subjective. One's understanding of the meaning of life's experiences is directly proportional to one's relationship and worship to God. In this way, worship now moves from being corporate worship to individual worship. Individual worship is vitally important in the life of the believer.

Individual worship in a corporate setting became pervasive in the Jesus People Movement (JPM). "The Jesus People Movement was a religious movement among White American youth in which the participants wed certain values of the 1960s American counterculture, namely hippiedom, together with values of Christianity, namely Pentecostalism." The phrase Jesus Movement, first appeared in an article written by Brian Vahon in *Life Magazine* in 1971 and was coined by Jack and Betty Cheetham. The Jesus People Movement took worship to another level as castaways and those who would otherwise fall through the cracks in traditional Christian denominations found God in unconventional ways. Their values, images, traditions and rituals were quite different from the contemporary churches. Hippies were finding God and their lives were being transformed by the power of the Holy Spirit. Unfortunately, many mainline churches were critical of the JMP and found it to be cultic. Bustraan states, "Without arguing for or against the anti-cult movements, its people and organizations filled a void and served a policing function in the arena outside the established church. While they have attempted to legitimize and delegitimize organizations based on their own evaluative criteria, many have testified to its benefit."[11]

The Renewal Movements were instrumental in changing the worship music of the contemporary church. Richard Bustraan states:

> Jesus People Movement music as a unique genre may have died off by the late seventies, but it should not be dismissed as a trivial, ephemeral expression of the JPM. Instead it was the harbinger of the transformation in Christian worship music that subsequently permeated Christian churches around the globe and the seed out of which the industry blossomed. The unbroken chain of continuity that can be traced from Jesus Music to Maranatha, Vineyard Music and to many other worship music derivatives of the present day shows this short lived genre to be one of the most enduring and influential contributions to global Christianity from the JPM.[12]

Lastly, a central issue about the idea of worship concerns the range of entities that can be worshiped. Ninian Smart ponders this matter in his work, The Concept of Worship, and asks "What range of entities can be objects of worship? Maybe there should be only one such entity, the true God. But that value-judgment differs from the issue of what entities it makes sense to worship." I found this discussion interesting and germane to the discussion of worship because the culture of narcissism and commercialism prevalent in our contemporary society has to be addressed. Individuals are coming to church today with varying allegiances of complicated values to people, places and things that impede their ability to embrace worship as contemporary liturgies encourage and expect. Therefore, intentional discovery of ways to introduce and encourage worship has to be explored and implemented. Scripture is clear that believers are to worship God in Spirit and in Truth. Expressions of worship as praying, bowing, lifting hands, kneeling, dancing, and singing may be presented in an imposing and abrasive manner which may be hard for some to embrace because it may suggests that everyone must worship this way. Value-judgment occurs when others do not respond in manners expected of them from other Christians. Smart further postulates that, "One does not learn the primary concept of worship by sweeping floors but by participating in and/or observing acts of worship such as singing hymns, addressing prayers to God and so on."[14]

The use of ritual and conventional meaning in worship has been a recurrent theme in the renewal movements. This indispensable factor for living an effective Christian life continues to be vitally important.

Worship (Axis 1): Healthy Spiritual Formation is accessed by intentional worship through *Spiritual Disciplines*. As multi-faceted beings (mind, body, & spirit) the Spiritual Dimension first and foremost is 'experiential.' It is not a mental assent. Worship is an experience. Spiritual Disciplines and Creative Acts of Worship for Axis 1: prayer, fasting, meditation, yoga, devotional, walking, reading, bible study, solitude, giving, singing, dancing, nature, use of one's physical body and senses.

ENDNOTES

[1]Ibid.

[2]Nathan Smith, Roots, Renewal and the Brethren (Pasedena, CA: Hope Publishing House, 1986), 125.

[3]Gordon Wakefield, An Outline of Christian Worship (Edinburgh, Scotland: T & T Clark LTD, 1998), 1.

[4]Wakefield, 153.

[5]Ibid., 77.

[6]Tom Smail, Andrew Walker and Nigel Wright, Charismatic Renewal: The Search for Theology (Great Britain: Society for Promoting Christian Knowledge, 1995), 109.

[7]Smail, 109.

[8]Esther Talbout Fenning, "Charismatic Renewal: Movement in Worship," St. Louis Post Edition, accessed August 19, 1994, 4, http://search.proquest.com.ezproxy.drew.edu.

[9]Graham Hughes, Worship as Meaning: A liturgical Theology for Late Modernity (United Kingdom: Cambridge University, 2003), 244-45.

[10]Turner, xvii.

[11]Richard Bustraan, The Jesus People Movement: A Story of Spiritual Revolution among the Hippies (Eugene, Oregon: Pickwick Publications, 2014), 171.

[12]Bustraan, 54.

[13]Ninian Smart, The Concept of Worship (Macmillan: St. Martin's Press, 1972), 3.

[14]Smart, 5.

CHAPTER SIX

SPIRITUAL FORMATION MOVEMENT (DISCIPLESHIP)

The Discipleship/Spiritual Formations was another major para church movement that contributed to the way we do discipleship. Included in this movement are groups as the Navigators, Worldwide Discipleship, and Campus Crusade for Christ, and authors such as Waylon Moofe, Gary Kuhne, Gene Getz, Richard Foster and Dallas Willard, who have underscored the importance of building up Christians and establishing personal spiritual disciplines.[1]

The Spiritual Formations Movement played a major role in cultivating renewed interests in the importance of spiritual development and discipleship. James C. Wilhoit states:

> Spiritual Formation is the task of the Church. Period. It represents neither an interesting, optional pursuit by the church nor an insignificant category in the job description of the body of Christ. Spiritual Formation is at the heart of its whole purpose for existence. The church was formed to form. Our charge, given by Jesus Himself, is to make disciples, baptizing them, and teach these new disciples to obey His commands (Matthew 28:19 – 20). The witness, worship, teaching, and compassion that the church is to practice all require that Christians be spiritually formed.[2]

Making disciples is therefore one of those indispensable factors for living an effective and victorious Christian life. Discipleship has to be an intentional aspect of the churches curriculum following the call to discipleship at the altar. Frank C. Senn states:

> Even so, it was Wesley who gave shape to the Methodist movement, and his spiritual insights provided its bedrock. His genius was to create a theological synthesis between the two major strands of English Protestant spirituality – Anglican holiness of intent and Puritan inward assurance – and apply it in the practical outworking of an accountable discipleship.[3]

To this end, spiritual formation has to be intentional. James C.

Wilhoit, a contributor of the Discipleship Movement, further states:

> Christian spiritual formation refers to the intentional communal process of growing in our relationship with God and becoming conformed to Christ through the power of the Holy Spirit. Spiritual Formation as a process, thereby implying that formation is a long-term, lifelong venture, and that it results from a multidimensional ministry, not just a technique of program.[4]

During the Spiritual Formations Movement many models for discipleship were introduced. Dallas Willard was a major contributor of this movement. Kieth Kettenring outlined two major concepts of personal transformation in Dallas Willard's model for discipleship. He states, "Dallas Willard's (2001) VIM (Vision, Intention, and Means) model provides a framework for this study of sanctificational growth. This model is utilized because it is a heuristic procedure that has the potential to describe santificational growth. It also provides support for the necessity for human participation in sancitificational growth. " Kettering goes on to define sanctification, "Sanctification relates to holiness as indicated by the translation of *hagios* in the New Testament. As a noun, it is translated "holy" or "sacred" while as a verb it is translated "make holy, consecrate, or sanctify." He further provides discussion on the distinction between positional sanctification, which occurs at the point of salvation, and progressive sanctification, which is the lifelong pursuit of holiness through a spiritual formation curriculum provided by the church. This point is poignant, because it provides insight into why some Christians go on to live effective and victorious Christian lives and others fall by the wayside of through the cracks.

Discipleship can best be likened to a learning process. Dallas Willard describes a disciple as an apprentice; "Someone who has decided to be with another person, under appropriate conditions, in order to become capable of doing what that person does or to become what that person is." Ernest Best uses the teachings found in the Gospel of Mark to expound on this process. He states:

> Followers is indeed the characteristic word which Jesus uses
> to men. 'Follow me' is the challenge to those who would be
> his disciples (1:17, 1:20. 2:14). The word 'follow' implies that
> the one who says it is in motion, and Mark depicts Jesus in
> motion in the accounts of the call of disciples. Throughout
> the Gospel the word 'follow' is used almost exclusively in the
> reference to the disciples of Jesus.[8]

Eugene Peterson echoes this fact and describes this process of
following Jesus as 'a long obedience'. He states:

> That men and women who believingly follow Jesus (what we
> commonly call "the Christian life" or Christian "spirituality")
> are best guided and energized by a fusion of Scripture and
> prayer. For as long as enthusiasm for Christian "spirituality"
> accelerates without an equivalent commitment to its means,
> nothing much is going to come of it.[9]

Suzanne Johnson echoes this fact when she states:

> Christian spiritual formation is a matter of becoming the
> song that we sing, the Story we tell. We are to become the
> living texts of Christianity. Its very intent is formation, not
> information. Our task is to let the Story so live through us
> that we are transformed to be as the Story is. The process of
> change is understood as sanctification or conversion.[10]

The conversion process ushers new believers into a journey of
spiritual development that provided Christian identity and spiritual
formation. Stephen Happel states:

> The prime spontaneous expression of our turning toward
> God is the individual that we are, the whole person directing
> his or her life toward the One who love us. In the New

Testament communities, symbols of Christian conversion were equally important. Symbol is the external expression of these inner changes. The public expression in the early community for this experience what Christians called the sacraments of the church, especially Baptism and the Eucharist. Eucharist and Baptism are first Christ's own symbolic self-expression. The Christian community took up the two symbols of the Eucharist and Baptism for their own process of self-identification.[11]

These foundational truths are pillars of the Christian faith and are significant in the disciple-formation process. Inherent in these traditions are principle of self-denial, as we follow Christ. Being baptized into the body of Christ served as an initiation rite for believers. The Eucharist is a life-long reminder of the sacrifice that Christ paid for our redemption and as we are invited to the table, we are admonished to take up our crosses, deny ourselves of carnal pursuits, and to follow Christ.

Richard Foster, another major contributor to the Spiritual Formations Movement, concurs with the process of following Christ as a life-long venture. He states:

This transforming work does not happen all at once and not completely perhaps. But it does happen. The old games of manipulation and control begin losing their appeal to us. Guile becomes less and less a pattern of our daily life. A new compassion rises up within us for the bruised and broken and the dispossessed. Indeed, it's a kind of well-reasoned concern of the well-being of all people, of all creation. We are becoming friends of Jesus.[13]

Daniel A. Helminiak further elaborates on the process of spiritual formation. He states:

A characteristic of spiritual development is that it involves the whole person; it entails personal integrity or wholeness. The specific intent of this insistence on wholeness or integrity is that the intrinsic dynamism toward authentic self-transcendence must not be forgotten when one speaks of human development. Thus, wholeness implies a growing self-consistency, a consistency within the whole. As humans follow the drive toward authentic self-transcendence and not only come to acknowledge what is really 'so' but also then decide and act appropriately on what they know, they effect changes not only in the external world on which they act but more importantly on themselves who are acting. They become as they do.[13]

Helminiak's discussion here on spiritual formation is vitally important to the discipleship process because it underscores the importance of self-investment. I believe healthy spiritual formation must be grounded in development of the self. Within the group dynamics of congregational life, David Augsburger states:

What makes witness authentic is neither the charismatic personality of an individual nor the perfection of a particular life; it is the presence of a community of witnesses who verify, validate, and authenticate their life together. Witness is a shared task, not an independent one. Such joint witnesses, when it is given in corporate life, makes both values and virtues visible. We live out our witnesses as a people; we find that a shared spirituality processes a sociological authenticity not possible for an individual on a private journey; we become a community of co-questors, not a world where each is pursuing her or his own quest.[14]

This provides a larger magnitude and scope for the discipleship process. Healthy Spiritual Formation and discipleship is an individual pursuit within a group dynamic. John Ackerman states:

Group growth requires individual growth. For the whole group to grow, every individual needs help to get in touch with his or her own individuality in God. For the group and the individual to be aligned with God's purposes, the group together needs to listen to God, to compare its spirit to the Holy Spirit. A group discernment process should not be limited to the spiritual elite who want to gather in exclusive groups with their like- minded colleagues. Adult education isn't just talking about scripture; its' helping people read the scripture and listen to and discern God's word addressed to them.[15]

This point is critical in the literature because, many denominations have hierarchical structures that divide and conquer. This stifles the discipleship process of the group and the individuals. One of the highlights of the Spiritual Formations Movement was the outpouring of the Holy Spirit among all the people. This outpouring crossed traditional barriers and empowered congregants as they heard from God. Of course, many denominations felt uncomfortable with this shift in the body of Christ.

As congregants were empowered by the Holy Spirit, they felt the need to challenge traditional barriers that heretofore kept them relegated to certain roles in the church. Richard Foster states:

Experiencing the inward reality liberates us outwardly. Speech becomes truthful and honest. The lust for status and position is gone because we no longer need status and position. We cease from showy extravagance not on the grounds of being unable to afford it, but on the grounds of principle. Our goods become available to others.[16]

This phenomenon in the discipleship process circumvents the spirit of narcissism that was prevalent then and which has pinnacled in the contemporary times in which we live today. Augsburger states:

In an age of narcissism the past is irrelevant, and the future will have to take care of itself. What matters to the narcissist are me and my satisfaction, safety, and security here and now. A spirituality that is focused on self-fulfillment, self-actualization, even self-transcendence is focused on the self and on the realization of the self's capacity to claim the higher reaches of human experience. This narcissism is evident in more than just occasional instances of immature spirituality. It is becoming the norm of both mainline and evangelical churches. In narcissistic faith, we focus on how God is meeting our needs and fulfilling our requests here and now. We no longer think of being part of God's purposes that stretch back into time and draw us toward His intentions for humanity.[17]

I agree with Augsburger and believe that this culture of narcissism has caused many to be lost from the flock. During the Spiritual Formations movement, the Holy Spirit attempted to eradicate this culture of narcissism, but human nature keeps it alive. Foster states:

Contemporary culture lacks both the inward reality and the outward life-style of simplicity. Because we lack a divine center our need for security has led us into an insane attachment to things. Courageously, we need to articulate new, more human ways to live. We should take exception to the modern psychosis that defines people by how much they can produce or what they earn. The Spiritual Discipline of simplicity in not a lost dream, but a recurrent vision throughout history. It can be recaptured today. It must be.[18]

One of the highlights of the Spiritual Formations Movement was the Campus Crusades for Christ Ministry. This ministry recaptured the fervor of simplicity mentioned by Richard Foster. God poured out the Holy Spirit among college campuses. Explaining how the ministry works Turner states:

Evangelical ecumenism remained very different from mainline Protestant ecumenism. Campus Crusade retained a seventeen-point statement of faith that began with an affirmation of biblical inerrancy and emphasized Jesus Christ as the only mediator between God and man (woman). Bill Bright recruited young evangelists who entered Greek houses that were anathema to most conservative Protestants, allowed several staff members to dress like hippies (also anathema) in the late 1960's and hired former executives to evangelize businessman and politicians.[19]

Thus, the Campus Crusade served to counter attack the culture of narcissism and wealth that consumed the world and the church. The foundational truths employed by this movement upon the discipleship process, had an internal and external impact. David Brown states:

> Discipleship is not simply a matter of individual relationship to Christ as lord or even of following His example, however indirectly, wherever it might lead. It also has a strong social dimension. In contemporary theology this is pursued overwhelmingly through reflection on eschatology, the realization of Christ's kingdom within this world 'at the end of the age', and our present contribution towards that goal.[20]

Discipleship does impact the 'social theory of change'; the underlying motives, principles, and guidelines which shape a ministries global outlook on discipleship and spiritual formation. Ackerman states:

> The pastors of America have metamorphosed into a company of shopkeepers and the shops they keep are churches. They are preoccupied with shopkeeper's concerns – how to keep customers happy, how to lure customers away from competitors down the street, how to package the goods so that the customers will lay out more money. The pastor's responsibility is to keep the community attentive to God. It is the responsibility that is being abandoned in spades. Pastors and leaders will need their own personal mission statements

and their own regular discipline to get in touch with God's dream for their ministry.[21]

This discussion provides a grim outlook on the vital role that pastors should play in the church. I believe God has called pastors to be leaders in the Body of Christ and to be His voice piece to the congregants. When pastors are relegated to just being shopkeeper's, the magnitude and scope of their role is diminished.

Church's mission statements and foundational truths play a major role in the discipleship process for individual spiritual formation and church growth. Suzanne Johnson records:

> By its very nature, the church is an ecology of spiritual care and guidance. Spiritual guidance includes training persons in the skills and disciplines ingredient to living the Christian Story. These are fundamentally the means by which the church itself participates in and initiates persons into the Realm of God.[22]

Teaching the fundamental truths of the Christian faith is an integral factor for healthy spiritual formation. Christian education is the vehicle used to provide new believers with those fundamental truths that will ground them and sustain them through the harsh realities of life. Johnson further states:

> Christian education can be defined as the dynamic, intentional process of teaching and learning through which the faith community is initiated into ever more faithful and complex participation in God's creative and redemptive activity in the world. It consists of intentional and lifelong processes through which Christian character receives distinctive shape and orientation over a lifetime and through which the church itself is more fully initiated into the Realm of God through instruction and praxis. Instruction refers to deliberate means whereby the faith community teaches the

Story (Scripture and tradition) and skills for critical inquiry into and faithful, critical revision of it. Praxis includes the practice (means of grace) that Wesley called works of mercy and justice.[23]

The Spiritual Formations Movement and its impact on the importance of discipleship continue to serve as vehicles for discovering the invaluable and indispensable factor for living an effective Christian life

Discipleship (Axis 2): Healthy Spiritual Formation is <u>fostered</u> through a teaching curriculum of *Foundational Truths* in Axis 2: fall of man, propitiation, atonement, adoption, redemption, predestination, salvation, reconciliation, justification, forgiveness, faith, grace, mercy, regeneration, spiritual identity, restoration, Holy Spirit, Spiritual fruit, Spiritual gifts, Spiritual warfare, sanctification, eschatology, resurrection

ENDNOTES

[1]Ib Ibid.

[2]James C, Wilhoit, Spiritual Formation as if the Church Mattered: Growing in Christ through Community (Grand Rapids, Michigan: Baker Academic, 2008) 15-16.

[3]Frank C. Senn, Protestant Spiritual Traditions (New York: Paulist Press, 1986), 217.

[4]Wilhoit, 23.

[5]Keith Kettering, The Sanctification Connection: An Exploration of Human Participation in Spiritual Growth (Lanham, Maryland: University Press of America, 2008), 5.

[6]Ibid., 6.

[7]Dallas Williard, The Divine Conspiracy: Rediscovering Our Hidden Life in God (San Francisco, CA: Harper Collins Publisher, 1998), 282.

[8]Ernest Best, Disciples and Discipleship: Studies in the Gospel According to Mark (Edinburgh, United Kingdom: T&T Clark LTD, 1986), 5.

[9]Eugene Peterson, A long Obedience in the Same Direction (Downers Grove, Illinois: InterVarsity Press, 2000), 203.

[10]Suzanne Johnson, Christian Spiritual Formation in the Church and Classroom (Nashville, TN: Abingdon Press, 1989), 103.

[11]Stephen Happel and James J. Walter, Conversion and Discipleship: A Christian Foundation for Ethics and Doctrine (Philadelphia, PA: Fortress Press, 1986), 17-18.

[12]Richard J. Foster, Sanctuary of the Soul: Journey into Meditative Prayer (Downers Grove, Illinois: InterVarsity Press, 2011), 148.

[13]Daniel Helminiak, Spiritual Development: An Interdisciplinary Study (Chicago, Illinois: Loyola University Press, 1997), 36.

[14]David Augsburger, Dissident Discipleship: A Spirituality of Self-Surrender, Love of God, and Love of Neighbor (Grand Rapids, Michigan: Brazos Press, 2006), 179.

[15]John Ackerman, Spiritual Awakening: A Guide to Spiritual Life in Congregations (Colorado Springs, CO: NavPress, 1993), 85.

[16]Richard J. Foster, Celebration of Discipline: The Path to Spiritual Growth (San Francisco, CA: Harper & Row, 1988), 80.

[17]Augsburger, 182-83.

[18]Foster, Celebration of Discipline, 80-81.

[19]Turner, 231.

[20]David Brown, Discipleship and Imagination: Christian Tradition and Truth (Oxford: Oxford University Press, 2000), 8.

[21]Ackerman, 84.

[22]Johnson, 121.

[23]Ibid., 143-44.

CHAPTER SEVEN
SMALL GROUPS / PASTORAL CARE MOVEMENT (FELLOWSHIP)

The Literature review also explored the Small Group/Pastoral Care Movement. It has been the task of the small group/pastoral care movement to refocus the church on **Fellowship** and caring relationships within the body. Like the other parachurch movements, the Small Group/Pastoral Care Movement comprised of many contributors and has enlightened the churches understanding of the importance of fellowship in the life of the Christian believer and the dynamics of small groups. The American Baptists, Disciples of Christ, Episcopalians, Lutherans, Methodists, Presbyterians, Southern Baptists, and United Church of Christ were among many of its contributors. The Korean cell-church model and organizations such as Touch Ministries, Serendipity, Care Givers, and Stephen's Ministry have shown us the value of using small groups and the importance of caring for individuals. The small group or pastoral care dynamic provided an atmosphere where developing believers, at varying points in their spiritual journey, could meet to discuss a plethora of open-ended agenda items that impacted their spiritual identity. Frederick Quinn states:

> The church was a place to speak out freely on social and political issues such as war, gun control, immigration, capital punishment, civil rights, and the place of women in society and/or the place of persons of same-sex orientation in the wider life of the community. Finally, it was a prayerful setting where members realized the sad cost of divisions, and the joy of a purposeful community gathering to happily proclaim the news of the 'goodly fellowship' in Christ. [1]

The small group dynamic facilitated pastoral care in the vital role of developing and implementing a community to achieve effective and purposeful fellowship for believers. Pastoral care, as we understand it today has evolved down through the centuries.

> Abstract concepts of pastoral care have been developed through the centuries under such labels as 'pastoral theology,' but these concepts have been powerless to create effective pastors. A Christian pastor is one who in his very

person and in his living relationships with people mediates something of the quality of being which is found in a larger measure in the revelation of Christ. In this living relationship there are reconciliation, forgiveness, and healing which reach below the struggles of human existence into the very core of man's being. Only the presence of the Holy Spirit will save a pastor from a mechanical imitation of the model presented by Jesus – with all of the destructiveness of such imitation. [2]

The small group movement created an atmosphere where pastoral care became a shared responsibility for the entire congregation. The evolution of pastoral care is important as it outlines the progress and failures of the movement. The small group dynamic or pastoral care underscores the importance of fellowship. Fellowship is an indispensable factor for Christian discipleship because it provides a safe environment for accountability and healthy spiritual formation. Pastoral care, traditionally centered around the pastor, which was a major part of the problem – both for pastoral self-care and parishioners. This resulted in a greater understanding of congregational helps and the development of small groups to assist in the pastoral care role. Carroll Wise states:

> Pastoral care is the art of communicating the inner meaning of the Gospel to persons at the point of their need. Thus pastoral care is not 'pastoral theology,' especially when this term denotes a set of principles for the conduct of a specific activity. Pastoral care is more a function than an activity, more a living relationship than a theory or interpretation, more a matter of being than of doing. [3]

Fellowship among developing Christian believers affords a healthy exchange of ideas and encourages everyone in the group to identify and explore their ministry gift(s). Stephen Seamands echoes this important point by stating:

> In the daily grind of ministry it's easy to forget whose

ministry it is. Although we desire to serve Christ and often ask Him for help, we assume that it's our ministry and we are the principal actors. Ministry, then, is not so much asking Christ to join us in our ministry as we offer Him to others; ministry is participating with Christ in His ongoing ministry as He offers Himself to others through us. [4]

This shared responsibility for healthy spiritual formation provides accountability in a loving and affirming environment. The small group movement grew as the Christian church gained greater insight into the importance of congregational care for its' potential members. Freddy Clark states, "God's people then are called to be imitators of God. The disciples of Jesus Christ are to make disciples. Disciples are made by sharing with all people the teachings of Jesus so that His church would be rooted in nothing but that which was received from Him." [5] The small group dynamic was later referred to by churches as hospitality. Carroll Wise later went on to liken hospitality to what he calls covenant making. He uses hospitality as a paradigm for covenant or the laying out of an ethical framework of justice and addressing issues of liberation. He states, "The covenantal notion that gives credence to the subject of hospitality is the covenant God has with God's people."[6] From this perspective, fellowship provides a paradigm useful for understanding church membership, accountability and healthy spiritual formation for new converts and potential members. As the small group movement evolved, many churches experienced growth in their membership rosters. This was particularly prevalent in the Korean Christian Church. In his address during a church conference Ryu Tong-shik stated:

The life of the church can be preserved and developed only through constant renewal. The church is the Body of Christ and at the same time is the community of believers. The renewal of the church is a natural manifestation of the nature of the church in the Holy Spirit. Therefore, renewal of the church is not the result of man's effort, but the fruit of the work of God in Jesus Christ through the Holy Spirit among believers who obey God.[7]

The Korean Church came to understand the importance of lay ministers and developed cell groups to assist in the evangelism and fellowship of new believers.

> The Korean church began to ask what the mission of the church is. In this endeavor also, diverse understandings were revealed. The conservative group emphasized church-centered, lay evangelism. The church-centered understanding of evangelism and mission culminated in 1965-66, in a National Movement of Evangelism with the slogan, 'Thirty Million Koreans for Christ,' under the leadership of Dr. Helen Kim, president of Ewha University.[8]

The development and utilization of cell groups were instrumental in providing effective pastoral care to a growing membership and facilitated healthy spiritual formation. Much of what is distinctive about contemporary Korean Christianity can be traced to the influence of early twentieth-century Protestant missionaries. They employed a fundamentalist form of Christianity which stressed the inerrancy of the Bible and inflexible ideas about morality. Ecklund states:

> However, Korean Christians made Christianity distinctively their own. They emphasized the Korean Confucian tradition of hierarchical relationships and the shamanist tradition of religious emotionalism. The rapid expansion in Korea occurred in a period of Japanese occupation, which provided a unique subversive and political context in which the Korean church thrived. By 1990 there were about 2,000 Korean churches in the United States, with one church for every 300-350 Korean immigrants. [9]

Rapid church growth was directly proportional to the ability of small groups to disseminate the gospel message, in ways that the larger group could not.

Yong-Do Lee was another contributor of the small group movement in the Korean church. He stressed the importance of a life of repentance, prayer, thanksgiving, love and sacrifice. "Whenever he had a chance, he urged the renewal of Christian thought and called for reform from the pulpit in order to awaken the lethargic Korean church."[10] Lee was heavily influenced by his Methodist heritage and understood renewal of the church was accomplished by the presence of the Holy Spirit. It is important to note that Lee overemphasized one's personal experience and this informed his hermeneutic. For this reason many orthodox Christians criticized Lee, but the contribution of the importance of healthy spiritual formation through the presence of the Holy Spirit was an invaluable ingredient in the pastoral care movement and its work.

The beginnings of **Pentecostalism**, with its characteristic practice of speaking in tongues as evidence of baptism by the Holy Spirit was established in the last days by Saint Mary Magdalena Tate, who is also an Apostle Elder of the Church, a mother, a light to the nations of earth. Saint Mary Magdalena Tate, the First Chief Overseer and true Mother in true holiness, established the **Church of the Living God, the Pillar** and **Ground of the Truth** in 1903. She was led by the Holy Spirit to go out into the world and preach the Gospel first at Steel Springs, Tennessee.[11] Pentecostalism is often associated with a revival beginning in 1906 at the Apostolic Faith Gospel Mission on Azusa Street in Los Angeles, California.

> Among zealous heirs of John Wesley's Methodism such longings were expressed in the language of 'Christian perfection' or 'holiness,' while Protestants of Calvinist background spoke more of 'the higher Christian life.' With their stress on the need for a special work of the Holy Spirit, these longings led to episodes where the Holy Spirit was thought to descend in a special way. [12]

Charles Parham and William Seymour were major contributors to the early history of Pentecostalism and are mentioned in the literature because of its impact on rapid church growth and the pastoral care movement.

> Once underway, the Pentecostal movement rapidly became a world-wide phenomenon. Over the last half of this century, the charismatic movement in Catholic, Lutheran, Presbyterian, Episcopal, and many other denominations expanded emphases on healing and other spiritual gifts borrowed from earlier Pentecostalism. Together, the Pentecostal and charismatic emphases upon experiencing the grace of God – especially upon sensing God through more intimate, less cognitive forms of worship – have influenced Protestants, Catholics, and even some Orthodox all over the world. [13]

The baptism of the Holy Spirit is an important factor in fellowship. Rick Warren, the author of Purpose Driven Church, and the senior pastor of Saddleback Church (megachuch) postulates:

> I believe it is because it [fellowship] symbolizes one of the purposes of the church: fellowship – identification with the body of Christ. As Christians we're called to belong, not just to believe. We are not meant to live lone-ranger lives; instead, we are to belong to Christ's family and be members of His body. Baptism is not only a symbol of salvation; it is a symbol of fellowship. [14]

Saddleback, whose membership exceeds 10,000 believers, implemented small groups and lay leaders to effectively facilitate healthy spiritual formation for this large membership. Warren believes small groups afford accountability and pastoral care for its membership. Small groups were also developed and implemented abroad in East and West Africa. They were called small Christian communities (SCCs). Speaking about Christian community, Jeanne Hinton agreed with Christopher Mwoleka in a 1991 Notre Dame consultation, "We share everything in common, we bring up our children together, we attend to the sick and elderly together. We grow bananas, keep cows and pigs and 'live by our own sweat.' The main purpose is to gain strength to serve in the wider community."[15] Hinton agreed with Mwoleka that the importance of fellowship in a community is an invaluable and indispensible factor for healthy spiritual formation. Hinton further stated, "This 'integrated community,' as it is called, has a particular task – to inspire and help in the formation of small Christian communities (SCCs). Typically a community comes together only once a week, meeting informally in the homes of members. [16] These informal small groups were the invaluable ingredient in shaping healthy spiritual formation in an affirming and loving context.

Through the fellowship that they demonstrate, the Small Group/ Pastoral Care Movement proclaimed to the world, this person is now one of us. We have each other for support. You are members of God's very own family and you belong in God's household with every other Christian. Warren states, "The church exists to provide fellowship for believers."[17] I concur with the words of Sondra Matthaei, another small group contributor, who concludes, "Being heard, being known, and being accepted are the characteristics of authentic relationships. When others accept us as we really are, we come to know ourselves in new ways."[18] The framework that pastoral care provides, affords believers the comforts of attaining spiritual identity in an atmosphere that facilitates healthy spiritual formation.

> Hearing not only helps persons come to new self-awareness and self-understanding but also transforms community into communion. The word communion points to something deeper than our individual understanding of community. When we recognize that God is a participant in these relationships, community becomes communion as persons are heard, known, and accepted through the development of authentic relationships within our churches. Communion begins with hearing because it is in the hearing and then the listening that we find mutual authentic relationship. We are bound together in community by our shared life, but there is also room to celebrate the unique gifts of each

member of that communion. And communion brings deeper meaning to our lives.[19]

This is the inherent power and strength of fellowship, within a loving and affirming community. The small group movement provided a healthy environment conducive for healthy spiritual formation which afforded accountability and oversight for developing Christian believers. Speaking about fellowship, Richard Cimino states:

It's difficult to remain a removed observer when it comes to the Roman Catholic charismatic movement. Charismatics, with their emotional, even ecstatic, worship, their close bond of fellowship, and their expressive affection, had a way of putting me in the middle of things. This prayer group is a real family. Like that small prayer group dwarfed by its mammoth parish, the Catholic charismatic renewal movement generated a more personalized and informal style of faith that spilled out from the prayer groups and large charismatic conventions to have a significant impact on the contemporary church. [20]

This reflection describes the impact of fellowship and the small group movement on the larger church traditions at that time. John Casteel echoes this sentiment and provides biblical foundation for fellowship when states, "Modern individualist pietism is simply not Biblical. We have somehow equated "personal" with "individualist" religion. The very concept of person, rightly apprehended, implies membership in a community. No personal being, Paul Tillich reminds us, exists without communal being. "There is no person without encounter with other persons. Persons can grow only in the communion of personal encounter."[21] In his discussion of small groups, he quotes Theodore O. Wedel, "This was the greatest religious experience of my life." [22] This qualitative statement is relevant as it rates the importance of fellowship and validates it as an indispensable factor for living an effective Christian life. John Casteel then poses an interesting question, "Redemptive experience in Christian fellowship – Is this not one of the most essential marks of what the very word "church" should mean when it manifests such basic New Testament images of the church as Body of Christ and Fellowship of the Holy Spirit?"[23] Viewing fellowship from this perspective provides a schematic consistent with Scripture. "From whom the whole body fitly joined together and compacted by that which every joint supplieth, according to the effectual working in the measure of every part, making increase of the body unto the edifying of itself in love." (Ephesians 4:16). Membership in a local church provides wonderful fellowship which strengthens whole Body of Christ. A healthy local church is one that understands the importance of fellowship and creates a loving and affirming atmosphere conducive for accountability and healthy spiritual formation. The impact of fellowship among Christendom is invaluable for healthy spiritual formation. Small groups continue to be a vibrant and vital factor for developing healthy Christians. John Casteel states:

> You cannot by organization lead a person into a relationship with God – you must begin where a man is and help to awaken God within him. Something more than good preaching and teaching was needed. Modern man needs to find a vocabulary by which he can communicate religious ideas and feeling to another. He must have an experience of God as well as possess knowledge about God. Jesus had shared intimately religion as a way of life with a small band of disciples. John Wesley began his great Methodist movement with the Methodist "meeting." I was certain that this was the direction in which to move – the power of a small group. [24]

The universal church of Jesus Christ has always been in the process of renewal. Nothing remains static. Nathan Smith states:

> Families grow and change as children reach maturity, the elders die off, and new members are added through marriage and birth. So churches are never static because

there are new dynamics to contend with. There is a seducing tendency for faith to be pulled toward a rigid and formal religion. Fortunately, God, in His providence, enters this cycle and breathes new life into His people. Where new wine is made, the old forms and structures simply yield. [25]

John Patton in his book, From Ministry to Theology, provides a critical reflection of the group dynamic between the ministry and the community. He states:

> The ministry group develops a sense of community among the members, facilitated by an initial bracketing out of critical responses to what was shared. As relationships have developed brackets are gradually removed so that conceptualization, critique, and objectification become appropriate responses as the groups move from reflection on pastoral event to theological reconstruction. [26]

This critical reflection is important for the Lay Renewal Movement because it parallels the movement with the dynamism of church growth and membership patterns. Patton utilizes the work of anthropologist Victor Turner, in his studies of developing communities to understand the more sophisticated community of the church. He states:

> Turner uses the term communitas to identify a rudimentary structured and relatively undifferentiated community of equal individuals who submit together to the authority of a "ritual elder," a leader having been given authority by the larger community, tribe, or, in our case, religious group. Communitas has an existential quality involving the whole person in relation to other persons. [27]

This discussion on group dynamics underscores the importance on the evolution of individual church cultures and their impact on the spiritual formation process. This quality of the group dynamic is important in the **fellowship** of believers as it has allowed the movement to progress over time and maintained consistency of foundational truths and church traditions as the leadership changed.

Fellowship (Axis 3): Healthy Spiritual Formation is reinforced by its' natural progression to Axis 3 for healthy socialization and accountability within a loving and affirming community. In Axis 3: Mission & Vision Statements, Affirmation of Faith, *Traditions* (services, communion, water baptism, ethics, tithes, disputes, marriage, baby dedications, funerals/death), *Governance* (pastors, elders, deacons, trustees, board, ministers, overseers, lay leaders), *Fellowships* (Sunday service, Bible study, Sunday school, small groups, AA/NA, social calendar), membership.

From this perspective, the small group dynamic, transcended denominational barriers. People gathering in small groups and sharing hopes, experiences and struggles were instrumental in providing a safe haven for healthy spiritual formation.

ENDNOTES

[1]Frederick Quinn, *Building the "Goodly Fellowship of Faith": A History of the Episcopal Church in Utah, 1867-1996* (Logan, Utah: Utah State University Press, 2004), 272.
[2]Carroll A. Wise, The Meaning of Pastoral Care (New York: Harper & Row Publishers, 1966), 1.
[3]Wise, 8.
[4]Stephen Seamands, Ministry in the Image of God (Downers Grove, Illinois: IVP Books, 2005),
[5]Freddy James Clark, Hospitality: An Ecclesiology Practice of Ministry (Lanham, Maryland: Hamilton Books, 2007), 41.
[6]Ibid., 61.
[7]Boo-Woong Yoo, Korean Pentecostalism Its History and Theology (Frankfurt am Main: Verlag Peter Lang, 1988), 157.
[8]Yoo, 158.

[9]Elaine Howard Ecklund, Korean American Evangelicals: New Models for Civic Life (Oxford: Oxford University Press, 2006), 9.

[10]Ung Kyu Pak, Asian Thought and Culture: Millennialism in the Korean Protestant Church (New York: Peter Lang Publishing, Inc, 2005), 148.

[11]The Constitution Government and General Decree Book, p.4

[12]Mark A.Noll, Turning Points: Decisive Moments in the History of Christianity (Grand Rapids: Michigan, 2000), 299-300.

[13]Ibid., 300.

[14]Warren, Purpose Driven Church, 105.

[15]Jeanne Hinton, Walking in the Same Direction: A New Way of Being Church (Geneva, Switzerland: World Council of Churches, 1995), 22-23.

[16]Ibid., 23.

[17]Warren, Purpose Driven Church, 106.1.

[18]Sondra Higgins Matthaei, Formation in Faith: The Congregational Ministry of Making Disciples (Nashville: Abingdon Press, 2008), 3.1.

[19]Ibid., 6-7.

[20]Richard Cimino, Trusting the Spirit: Renewal and Reform in American Religion (San Francisco: Jossey-Bass, 2001), 13.

[21]John L. Casteel ed., The Creative Role of Interpersonal Groups in the Church Today (New York: Association Press, 1968), 46.

[22]Ibid.,42.

[23]Ibid., 61.

[24]John L. Casteel, Spiritual Renewal Through Personal Groups (New York: Association Press, 1957), 30-33.

[25]Nathan Delynn Smith, Roots, Renewal and the Brethren (Pasedena, CA: Hope Publishing House, 1986), 2

[26]John Patton, From Ministry to Theology (Nashville: Abingdon Press, 1990), 50-51.

[27]Patton, 52-53.

CHAPTER EIGHT
LAY RENEWAL MOVEMENT (MINISTRY)

Elton Trueblood, Findley Edge, and David Haney, were the major contributors of the Lay Renewal Movement. This movement refocused the church on the **Ministry** of the Christian church.

The Lay Renewal Movement served to refocus the church on the Ministry of the Christian church.

> The thirty-five year history of the "lay movement" has been continually coordinated and encouraged by the World Council of Churches, and the Collaboration Committee is one current form of this encouragement. The World Collaboration Committee for Christian Lay Centres, Academies, and Movements for Social Concern is a network with the following purposes: 1) To establish channels of communication; 2) To develop programs as international studies, research, training courses, exchange of staff; 3) To offer consultative or advisory service on personnel; and 4) To develop relations with other agencies with particular concerns. [1]

The work of the ministry is both an individual and collective enterprise. This is a complex phenomenon and has been problematic for churches. Robert C. Worley, a contributor of the Lay Renewal movement states:

> The problem of understanding the membership in the church and ministry by clergy and laity is related to the turbulence in congregations. We must focus on the organizations and the methods of governance in these organizations as at least partial answer to this problem. There is wholeness to Christ's ministry which is not found normally in the church today. Congregations expect that the minister will "do it" – whatever the ministry is. Cultural conditioning, theological education, and personal style and proclivities have combined to produce both ministers and lay persons with expectations which are theologically heretical. [2]

This problem was the impetus for the Lay Renewal movement and the importance of laity involvement in the work of the ministry.

Lovett Weems Jr. and Tom Berlin states:

> Clergypersons sometimes feel that they have only two options: one is "faithfulness," with little regard for results, and the other is to adopt the "success" culture they see around them. But a third option is fruitfulness. Fruitfulness has as its goal not personal advancement or acclaim but the advancement of God's reign on earth. It seeks to shape the life and work of the congregation through a shared passion for its mission. [3]

Learning about the congregation, a churches history and mission, is important because it allows the leadership to bring the membership alongside them in the task of discovering God's will for the particular church and its' individual members. This is work. Marcene Marcoux suggests:

> Without a doubt movements entail work. Since individuals do not automatically embrace a program of renewal, there must be a basis for their support, and it is this ground that constitutes part of the present work of the movement; the process of legitimization. Legitimization is the crown jewel or reward one finds in discovering their ministry gift. It has been said that there are two (2) important days in one's life: the day they are born and the day they know why they were born. Legitimization is about discovering one's purpose in life. This indispensable factor circumvents countless years of wandering, experimentation and enticement to illicit behavioral patterns. The work of legitimization is complex and elaborate. [4]

Worley argues, "Most Legitimization is given to particular kinds of sacramental-priestly and pastoral functions. But in Protestantism there is little understanding and legitimization of kingly-governance or political leadership activities. A great deal of stress is created by those who use a political style rooted in feudal tradition."[5] This discussion of legitimization is important here because it provides the etiology of the problem with many churches that see church agencies as to be ruled autocratically, from the top down. This schematic does not invoke the fruitfulness of the entire membership, thus placing undue burden upon the clergy, while dismissing the membership. Members waste countless years because they are not supported in self-discovery of their purpose and ministry gifting. A healthy local church is one that understands the importance of assisting the members in discovering their ministry gift(s) and allowing them to use them in service to the Lord and others. This legitimization is empowering as it solidifies one's purpose for living. It also helps to offset idleness which is an arena for illicit temptations to flourish.

The Lay Renewal Movement sought to recapture the biblical understanding of the ecclesia and the membership gifts. Findley B. Edge, a major contributor of the Lay Renewal Movement states, "Anyone even casually related to the church is aware that it has come upon hard times. This is a rather strange phenomenon because the church today has more members than ever before to do its work, and they are better educated than they have ever been. But in spite of this, church work is declining in many areas."[6] He concludes that the doctrine of the priesthood of all believers is God's call to ministry. God ordained to accomplish His redemptive purpose in the world through 'a people' called to be the ministers. That means, "The primary responsibility for God's ministry in the world is the responsibility of the laity and not the clergy."[7] This legitimization of the laity was the strongest impact of the Lay Renewal Movement. Edge believed that while in church, the believer should study, worship, and open their lives to the Spirit of God. "When the worship, study, planning, and equipping are completed, they go out to invade the world for God; In stores, shops, offices, factories, homes, farms, each expresses his ministry."[8] To this end, Edge believes that God's basic call is a call to ministry.

Elton Trueblood, another major contributor of the Lay Renewal Movement, states, "All Christians are called to the ministry regardless of their particular secular occupations." James Newby once stated of Trueblood, "Elton is still, perhaps, the most quoted religious leader in the country." [10] He quotes one of Elton's most notable writings on wholisitic Christianity:

> The only way in which a person may achieve relative unity of life is by dedication to something outside himself, to which he gives such loyal devotion that the self is forgotten in the process. The competing parts of our lives, which cannot unite themselves, are then united because of a unity of direction, when all the parts point one way. The ancient truth is that the health of the self comes, not by concentrating oneself, but by such dedication to something outside the self, that self is thereby forgotten. [11]

Findley Edge further explored the will of God and the Christian life in his work, A Quest for Vitality in Religion: *A Theological Approach to Religious Education.* He attempted to answer the question, "What does it mean to be Christian?" In answering this question, he employed Matthew 7:18-20; Jesus declared that tree is known by its fruit. "A good tree cannot bring forth evil fruit; neither can a corrupt tree bring forth good fruit. Wherefore by their fruits ye shall know them. Edge pondered the nature of this fruit and was convinced that Jesus gave a clear answer: Fruit comes in doing "the will of my Father which is in heaven." (v. 21) Edge concluded, the concept of "the will of God" provides the framework in which the mission and the ministry are to be accomplished.

Findley Edge, Elton Trueblood and other contributors of the lay Renewal Movement understood the importance of each individual believer discovering their ministry gift and purpose in the Body of

Christ. Edge posits:

> Herein is a basic part of the problem. The preaching and
> the teaching that has been done in the churches have led
> people to accept Christianity in terms of such generalized
> ideals that almost anyone can agree with them. But these
> people have not known how these generalized ideals are to
> be implemented and expressed in specific situations.[12]

Jim Wallis echoes this point when he states:

> I just seek to be a person who lives what I believe and who
> lives what God has asked me to live. It's clear to me that
> God ask me to love. That means I have to offer food to
> the person who's hungry, clothes to the person who has no
> clothes; I have to welcome the stranger in my midst, and
> I have to work for the day when those needs, when those
> deprivations, those injustices won't be. It's an outpouring of
> myself more than anything else. I believe I am to love, and
> in so doing here I am.[13]

Edward O'Connor describes what it is to live out the mandate of
Christian love in ministry. He states:

> It is a sudden gift of love taking hold of our whole being as a
> sensible fire rather than as a light. The whole life of the being
> that has undergone such an experience is now transformed
> into a continuous song of love: the melos amoris, which
> gives a tone to everything we know, feel or do. The whole
> matter of a Christian spiritual life is an experience of love,
> and goes far as to acknowledge also that it should permeate
> our entire being, including our bodily sensibility.[14]

D. Elton Trueblood states:

> One of the blessings of maturity which is seldom sufficiently

recognized is that of genuine humility. In early life there is a strong tendency to suppose that we have all of the answers, but some experience of life can cure this malady. One mark of intellectual growth is the recognition that there are no simple answers. In the logic of living, gratitude is the normal result of humility. In this fashion, gratitude can become a way of life. The greatest blessing of maturity is that gratitude may transcend the single occasion, to become both habitual and continuous.[15]

The Lay Renewal Movement refocused the churches attention on the importance of ministry, fruitfulness, and purpose. It is the critically important for the church to continue to provide agency for this endeavor. "I believe the greatest tragedy in life is not death. The greatest tragedy in life is life without a purpose." ~ The Late Dr. Myles Monroe, Bahamas Faith Ministries International, founder and senior pastor.

Ministry (Axis 4): Healthy Spiritual Formation is demonstrated through ministry gifts within a loving and affirming community of Axis 4. *Ministry gifts* (preaching, teaching, counseling, hospitality, visitation, benevolence, evangelism, administration, liturgy). *Ministry roles* (pastors, elders, trustees, teachers, deacons, lay leaders, counselors, ushers, music ministry, audio, altar workers, intercessors, janitorial, floral guild, culinary, children's ministry, youth ministry, senior services, nursing care, pastoral aides, greeters, media, programming, clerical).

ENDNOTES

[1] World Council of Churches, Voices of Solidarity (Geneva, Switzerland: World of Council Churches, 1981), 13.

[2] Robert C. Worley, A Gathering of Strangers: Understanding the Life of Your Church, (Philadelphia, PA: Westminster Press, 1976), 99.

[3] Lovett H. Weems Jr. and Tom Berlin, Bearing Fruit: Ministry with Real Results (Nashville: Abingdon Press, 2011), xvi.

[4] Marcene Marcoux, Cursillo – Anatomy of a Movement: The Experience of Spiritual Renewal (NewYork: Lambeth Press, 1982), 192.

[5] Worley, 98.

[6] Findley B. Edge, The Greening of the Church (Waco, Texas: Word Books, 1971), 37-38.

[7] Ibid., 39.

[8] Ibid., 47.

[9] Elton Trueblood, While it is Day: An Autobiography (New York: Harper & Row Publishers, 1971), 84-85.

[10] James R. Newby, Elton Trueblood: Believer, Teacher, and Friend (San Francisco: Harper & Row Publishers, 1990), 160.

[11] Ibid, 163.

[12] Edge, A Quest For Vitality in Religion, 110-11.

[13] Jim Wallis ed., The Rise of Christian Conscience (New York: Harper & Row Publishers, 1987), 17-18.

[14] Edward D. O'Connor ed., Perspectives on Charismatic Renewal (Notre Dame, London: University of Notre Dame Press, 1975), 126.

[15] D. Elton Trueblood, Essays in Gratitude (Nashville: Abingdon Press, 1982), 17-18.

Chapter Nine

Church Growth Movement (Evangelism)

The Church Growth movement was founded by Donald McGaravan in the 1950's. The Church Growth movement refocused the churches attention on the importance of evangelism and missions. The Church Growth movement was a parachurch movement that placed value on the church having a broader global perspective and marketplace transformation. While studying growing churches in India, McGaravan noted several important sociological factors: Cultural adaptation of worship and preaching; and the homogeneous unit principle. Describing McGaravan's work, Robb Redman states:

> People are more receptive to the gospel in the company of their peers."[16] He further records, "McGaravan's student C. Peter Wagner discovered that many of the mentor's principles worked in a North American setting as well. The movement is influential and controversial. Wagner has taught and mentored many of the leading seeker church pastors in his courses at Fuller Theological Seminary, notably the late John Wimber, Rick Warren and Walt Kallestad. As the megachurch became more prominent in the 1980's and 1990's, the church growth movement's practical focus attracted many pastors and church leaders to conferences and courses on how to build a growing church.[17]

The criticism of the movement has been its' de-prioritization of the place of worship in the service. This phenomenon has caused many of the adherents to reduce it liturgy to 'seeker-sensitive' strategies. Seeker-sensitive refers to those congregants who are not yet believers, but who come to churches seeking to know who God is and what the Christian message is all about. Seeker-sensitive people are looking for purpose in life, wholeness of person and answers to life/death issues. Redmann states, "But for a church that attempts a seeker-sensitive worship service, the issue of participation is critical. A key assumption of seeker service advocates is that seekers don't want to participate actively in worship."[18] For the purposes of this project I will focus my attention on the positive impact of the movement. The positive impact of the movement centers around having a global perspective and an understanding of marketplace transformation; 'Light driving away the darkness.' The most important feature of the Church Growth theory is that, "It uses the social sciences of sociology, ethnography, and demographics to understand how people live, think and feel; it challenges church leaders to pay attention to the environmental factors." [19]

Church growth has much to do with evangelism and the church's understanding of the Great Commission to go and make disciples. Win & Charles Arn, other major contributors to the church growth movement, states, "While the church has grown – and there are more Christians today than ever before in the history of the world – there is still a vast unfinished task."[20] They further argue:

Most approaches to mass and local church evangelism today have a significant common shortcoming. Attention is centered around, and success judged according to, the goal of "getting a decision." That brief verbal commitment is seen as the ultimate response to the Great Commission. Unfortunately, there is often a great gap between getting a decision and making a disciple. [21]

Donald McGaravan states:

It is impossible to ignore the call to evangelism, for it is being raised in so many quarters of the world. As we have studied evangelism in its ecumenical setting, we have been burdened by a sense of urgency. We have recaptured something of the spirit of the apostolic age, when the believers went everywhere preaching the word.[22]

This impetus for the church growth movement refocused the churches on the importance of evangelism. McGaravan states, "Evangelism proclaims Christ and persuades men to become His disciples and responsible members of His Church. Ideally it is His Church only. To some extent I agree that evangelism is "a function of expectancy."[23] The value of the Church Growth movement rests in its ability to circumvent isolationism that is prevalent in many denominations and local church parishes. Many local churches know very little about the world around them. They are not interested in the community, social issues, educational systems, law enforcement, local government or politics. This is a major problem, because the church cannot be the church if it is an island to itself. The Great Commission compels us to go into the world. This is a literal imperative, not just a suggestion. The world cannot hear the gospel of Jesus Christ, if the church confines itself to their four walls.

C. Peter Wagner, emphatically states, "The positive dimension of the Christian's involvement in the world is found in our Lord's high-priestly prayer in John 17. The principal objective of sending believers into the world is that the world might believe. (v. 12)."[24] He believes the main responsibility of the church is the preaching of the gospel or kerygma. He states, "But even the announcement of the kerygma is only a means to another end. The objective, according to the Great Commission, is to make disciples and baptize them, which indicates that they should become members of the church (Matt. 29:19)."[25] Evangelism is a challenge for many churches as it requires them to come out from beyond their sacred four walls and into the community. Robert Tuttle states simply:

> I have often said that the presentation of the gospel can be described in two words – hard work. The more detailed work of discipleship (usually within community) must then lead to the more careful analysis of peoples in culture. To communicate at one level does not mean that the work of evangelism has been done.[26]

Evangelism is the culmination of healthy spiritual formation because it understands that the Kingdom is present where the church is.

Developing a global perspective and embracing marketplace transformation is the sign of a healthy Christian and hence is an indispensable factor for living an effective Christian life.

Understanding that 'the world is the Lord's and the fullness thereof' is an empowering ingredient. Donald McGaravan echoes this sentiment when he states:

> Church growth follows where Christians show faithfulness in finding the lost. The purpose is not to search, but to find. The goal is not to send powdered milk or kindly messages to the son in the far country. It is to see him walking in through the front door of his (her) father's house. It never takes place among the indifferent or rebellious.[27]

I concur with his critique that:

> Since church growth has been born in an inter-denominational milieu and taught to missionaries and ministers of many theological persuasions, naturally therefore to denominational theologians church growth looks inadequately theological. They consider it as method not theology. Baptismal regenerationists complain that church growth does not believe in baptism. Some Calvinists complain that church growth overlooks the sovereignty of God. Pentecostals tend to feel that church growth gives insufficient emphasis to the Holy Spirit. Those fighting for social justice like to say that church growth men teach cheap grace. Those interested in liturgy find that church growth says very little about liturgy.[28]

The response to the critics by the church growth movement is to build theology with growth concepts as to the urgency and authority of evangelism into it. The biblical precedent lies in the common interpretation of the Great Commission (Matt 28:19-20). "The mission of the church is quite literally, be equipped bluntly or subtly, to "scare hell out" of people. The individual, convicted of his sin, accepts Jesus Christ as his Lord and Savior."[29] While this discussion underscores many of the inherent dangers in the church growth movement, it doesn't dismiss the importance of evangelism as an invaluable ingredient for healthy spiritual formation.   In many denominations, this 'call to discipleship' is the main focal point for evangelism. Holmes states however:

> I call this a method of recruitment because the intermediate objective – assuming the ultimate objective is the wholeness of the person of his union with God – is to get the individual's name one way or another in the book of life (sometimes confused with the parish register).   Recruitment is the obvious answer in many mainline churches to the decline in church membership roles from 1968 on.[30]

This is problematic because is somehow makes numbers dominate the evaluation of Christian outreach and evangelism. Holmes and his contribution to the church growth movement refocused the mission of the church: to win individuals not by recruiting them into heaven but the aim was to free people from what enslaved them and to establish a new society. "The Christian mission in liberation theology assumes the presence of God in all of life. It enables us to work apart from the trappings and deceptions of religion."[31] It moves us to a place where social reform is not relegated to just the politicians, but we understand the value that the church plays in the marketplace. Understanding and embracing the mandate of evangelism pushes us to be social reformers. We understand that we are not free, until we are **all** free. The church growth movement gained momentum as it understood theology of liberation and missions.

The Wesleyan Movement has been responsible for explosive church growth around the world for the last two centuries. Donald McGaravan and George Hunter III states:

Today's church growth movement has rediscovered church growth. The missionary movement, which at the outset was focused exclusively on carrying out the Great Commission, and based solidly on the ancient conviction that the Gospel was for all people, became excessively concerned with other things than communicating that Gospel to the peoples of the earth. So the assumption evolved that social action and the changing of social structures were basic functions of the Christian mission. Even as evangelism became more and more "renewal," an effort to make existing Christians better Christians.[32]

As the movement gained momentum, the church grew in magnitude and scope and facilitated healthy spiritual formation for those who embraced it. Christians gained greater insight into the Great Commission and it informed a more focused and scripturally sound mission and vision statement for local parishes. David Smith concludes:

> What is clear by now is that both the concept of mission as a one-way movement from Christendom to the unevangelised world, and the structures devised at the close of the eighteenth century to facilitate that movement, have been overtaken by historical developments that render them increasingly irrelevant and redundant. To fail to make this distinction between mission, as the abiding obligation and mark of the church, and missions, signifying specific historically conditioned institutions created to advance the cause of the kingdom in particular cultural situations, is to risk being locked into an obsolete model and so to be condemned to increasingly futile and frustrating activity. [33]

It is this frustrating and futile redundancy that has caused many local churches to die. They die from the inside-out because their initial fervor for evangelism got lost in tradition, legalism and customs. Seeker-sensitive individuals are not attracted to this kind of environment. This environment becomes a safe haven only for the current membership. But for a church to grow and to continue to grow, it has to reproduce itself. If there is no reproduction going on, this church will eventually die, when the membership gets older and naturally begin to die. This has been the detriment of many local churches because of their inability to embrace newer strategies to make itself relevant to a narcissistic culture, which is only concerned with self. So seekers leave the world and come into the church, only to find the same environment that it is running from, present there. The environment of producing mega-churches and focusing on materialism is a self-absorbed church, where individual care can be easily overlooked.

The church growth movement understood and attempted to respond to this dilemma. Peter Wagner, a pioneer in the church growth movement placed a great value on the individual effort of every believer to play their part in evangelism efforts. He states:

> In order to evangelize the world more effectively in our generation, I believe that many evangelicals need to get their heads out of the clouds when it comes to pronouncements about the degree of involvement that the average Christian ought to have in active evangelistic work. There are certain basic things that we need to recognize. For one thing every true Christian has got to be in tune with God who is 'not willing that any should perish, but that all should come to repentance' (2 Peter 3:9).[34]

The impact of the church growth movement continues to be felt among the churches throughout the world and is evidenced by ecumenism. A major event in this endeavor was a national ecumenical consultation sponsored by the Episcopal Church in November 1978 near Detroit.

> The Detroit Report opens with a strong statement that the Lord of the church through Scripture calls His church to make visible unity He has given to the church. In this communion of communions, churches recognize one

another's members and ministers, share eucharistic fellowship, acknowledge membership in the catholic church throughout time and space, engage in a common proclamation of the gospel, and share a mutual trust and dedication to the needs of the world. [35]

Evangelism allows the 'church organism' to have global impact – light driving out the darkness; and transformation in the marketplace. This global perspective serves to circumvent the church from isolationism and being self-absorbed in the sole survival of its' four walls. The impact of the church growth movement continues to evolve as the church searches for relevancy in the community and the world at large.

Evangelism (Axis 5): Healthy Spiritual Formation is <u>fulfilled</u> as it extends to the world for global impact and market place transformation. Areas include: Missions, outreach, street ministry, revivals, prison ministry, businesses, train & bus stations, food banks, clothing drives, housing, job readiness, voter registration drives, community activism, ecumenical alliances, PTA's and gang violence intervention.

ENDNOTES

[16]Robb Redman, The Great Worship Awakening: Singing a New Song in the Postmodern Church (San Fancisco, CA: Jossey-Bass Publishers, 2002), 12.

[17]Ibid.

[18]Redman, 19.

[19]Ibid., 13.

[20]Win Arn & Charles Arn, The Master's Plan for Making Disciples (Grand Rapids, Michigan: Baker Books, 1998), 8.

[21]Win Arn & Charles Arn, 12.

[22]Donald McGaravan, Eye of the Storm: The Great Debate in Mission (Waco, Texas: Word Publishers, 1972), 41.

[23]Ibid., 57.

[24]C. Peter Wagner, Latin American Theology: Radical or Evangelical? (Grand rapids, Michigan: Wm B. Eerdmans Publishers, 1970), 105.

[25]Ibid.

[26]Robert G. Tuttle, Jr., Can We Talk? Sharing Your Faith in a Pre-Christian World (Nashville; Abingdon Press, 1999), 17.

[27]Donald A. McGaravan, Understanding Church Growth , Fully Revised (Grand Rapids, Michigan: Wm B. Eerdmans Publishers, 1970), 5.

[28]McGaravan, Understanding Church Growth , Fully Revised, 7-8.

[29]Urban T. Holmes, Turning to Christ: A Theology of Renewal and Evangelism (New York: Seabury Press, 1981), 114.

[30]Ibid., 115.

[31]Holmes, 117.

[32]Donald McGaravan, and George G. Hunter III, Church Growth: Strategies that Work, Creative Leadership Series, (Nashville: Abingdon Press, 1980), 14-15.

[33]David Smith, Mission After Christendom, (London: Darton, Longman & Todd, 2003), 116.

[34]C. Peter Wagner, Your Spiritual Gifts Can Help Your Church Grow (Glendale, CA: Regal Books, 1974), 176.

[35]William G. Rusch, Ecumenism: A Movement Toward Church Unity (Philadelphia: Fortress Press, 1985), 96.

FINDINGS

The methodology for this project began with a thorough review of the literature in an effort to ascertain those indispensable factors that lead to effective Christian living. Those indispensable factors were identified as: Worship, Discipleship, Fellowship, Ministry and Evangelism. This review was followed by the creation of an anonymous, empirical, objective self-report survey that was distributed to four selected churches membership to determine if the respondents were familiar with those five indispensable factors and its' impact on their spiritual formation. A total of eighty (80) individuals completed the survey. 85% of the respondents reported that they were provided an understanding of the importance of **Worship** through the discipleship lessons offered. 84% of the respondents reported that they were provided an understanding of the importance of Ministry through the discipleship lesson offered them. 76% of the respondents reported that they were provided an understanding of the importance of **Discipleship** through the discipleship lessons offered them. 89% of the respondents reported that they were provided an understanding of the importance of **Fellowship** through the discipleship lessons offered them. 80% of the respondents reported that they were provided an understanding of the importance of **Evangelism** through the spiritual formation lessons offered them. This quantitative data from the selected churches supported the literature and validated those five factors as indispensable to the discipleship process. Consequently, the five factors were integrated into the spiritual formation model created for Chosen Generation Community Church.

Special attention was given to the respondents understanding of the spiritual formation processes offered at their churches and how they fostered spiritual development. 84% of the respondents reported that discipleship lessons for continued spiritual growth were offered at their churches. 68% of the respondents provided qualitative feedback when asked to describe how the Discipleship lessons improved their spiritual development.

PAC examined the path to discipleship from the initial "call to discipleship" through the spiritual formation process that selected churches employed. 84% of the respondents reported that they were invited to participate in an Altar Call to Discipleship. 81% of the respondents reported that they understood the Call to Discipleship. PAC believes healthy spiritual formation responds favorably to a point in time moment when a decision is made to accept Jesus Christ as Lord and Savior and to follow Jesus. This moment in time establishes Christian identity and serves as a benchmark going forward. Perhaps for some it serves as the day they report being "born again." 86% of the respondents reported that their conversion was recognized and/or celebrated by their church. This data suggests that this recognition plays a part in legitimization and opens the door for accountability. 76% of the respondents reported that they were offered a new members class at their church. 79% of the respondents reported that the class provided them an understanding of their new Christian identity. 89% of the respondents reported that the discipleship lessons provided a clear path for healthy spiritual formation. This data suggests that healthy spiritual formation is augmented by a deliberate process that is clear and concise. Moreover, 86% of the respondents reported that they were living an effective Christian life as a result of the lessons offered them. This was the most critical data, because it asks the respondents to assess their spiritual maturity based upon a deliberate discipleship narrative. The Terms described effective Christian living as a holistic lifestyle where mind, body and soul are in balance with a realistic understanding of fundamental truths of the faith. PAC believes this realistic understanding provides the needed magnitude and scope for developing Christians to weather the storms and vicissitudes of life.

PAC examined the respondents' knowledge of their churches adherence to its' Mission Statement. 88% of the respondents reported that they were aware of their church's Mission Statement. 84% of the respondents reported that their churches adhered to its' Mission Statement. This data is important and suggests that respondents are aware of their churches vision around missions and believe their churches are adhering to them. Perhaps inconsistencies between perception and reality can impact healthy spiritual formation, but this survey did not address that.

PAC examined the church's protocol to account for absenteeism. 79% of the respondents reported that their churches reached out to them when they were absent or away. PAC particularly was exploring if there were any inconsistencies in protocol which would allow believers to fall away. Unfortunately, this question did not allow us to effectively ascertain that information, because the methodology did not include information from those who did in fact fall away or stopped attending services. The methodology was not equipped to match membership rosters over time, against present membership. The methodology was also limited by those who freely responded to the request to participate in the survey. This was an inherent bias in the sampling because of the selection process employed. Three out of the four selected churches reported poor record keeping in regards to membership rosters and had no way to account for those who stopped attending.

The survey results were used to create a working Spiritual Formation Model that would be implemented at the Chosen Generation Community Church in Plainfield, New Jersey. The created Spiritual Formation Model effectively integrated those five indispensable factors of Worship, Discipleship, Fellowship, Ministry and Evangelism into a schematic that had at its' Core, the existence of God. The model depicts three Tiers of development in the formation process - self, other and God. There is a natural progression from Tier 1 through to Tier 3. The model consists of three (3) components: one core, five axes, and three tiers. It provides a clear path from the initial call to discipleship through spiritual maturity.

The genius of the schematic is that any believer could easily pinpoint where they are in the process. The schematic does assume everyone is at the same place and it allows everyone to grow at a pace comfortable for them. It allows the believer to understand their strengths and weaknesses. Healthy spiritual formation is accessed and fostered through self-development by spiritual disciplines and foundational truths. Healthy spiritual formation is reinforced and demonstrated as a natural progression to "the other" within a loving and affirming community. Healthy spiritual formation is fulfilled as it extends to the world for global impact and marketplace transformation.

It was noted that PAC's understanding of a Discipleship Model was positively impacted by this project. Some of the glaring differences noted among the selected churches were as follows: Church A - reached its' climax or pinnacle of growth; Church B - was a dying church; Church C - was a church in peril; and Church D - was a healthy church that reached its' optimum potential. It was noted that none of the selected churches had a mechanism to monitor membership retention.

The methodology and project design was clear and concise. The methodology did not have a mechanism to retrieve feedback from those who terminated their membership at the selected churches, or who were absent without leave. Other limitations to the methodology were the inherent biases due to the demographic makeup of those who responded to the survey. Therefore inferences could only be made to populations with similar demographics. Surveying a larger and more diverse sample would be a recommended improvement to the methodology. This research opened up a way to discuss shortcomings and strengths of the spiritual formation processes of urban churches and offers them suggestions on what to work on. In addition, follow-up procedure to re-visit the survey could improve upon the initial findings.

My observations regarding this project were multi-faceted. Mostly I was impressed with the fact that the selected church's leadership and congregants wanted to grow spiritually. I observed that many of the church's infrastructure and polity impeded growth and was not friendly to change. Therefore, any plan of action need to be preceded with a seminar on the importance of implementing change. It is vitally important that Mission Statements utilize user-friendly language that connects theology and theory to praxis.

Personally, I grew emotionally and spiritually through this process as I viewed the project as a life's body of work becoming unraveled through self-discovery and the group dynamic. The magnitude and scope of the project opened up my way of thinking concerning spiritual formation, particularly as the laity is involved. It renewed my enthusiasm for Christianity and its' ability to answer humanity's inner quest for purpose, wholeness and direction. In a culture that has been invaded with apathy and narcissism, I believe Christianity still stands as a vibrant antidote. The greatest value of this project was an increased awareness around the importance of bridging the gap to account for those lost in the cracks or fallen by the wayside. My awareness was heightened as I integrated Tier 1 work into the therapeutic milieu at Chosen Generation Community Corp. The testimonials in the Preface describes how Tier 1 was integrated into activities of daily living. Tier 1 was able to navigate respondents through marital issues, family issues, substance abuse issues and spiritual distress. Tier 1, because of its spiritual nature, was able to replace anxiety and strife with peace, purpose, direction, understanding, resolve and joy. I was able to witness respondent's preparedness to proceed to Tiers 2 & 3 as a result of being grounded in Tier 1. Tier 1 heightens awareness and empowers respondents with a strength they did not possess prior to crises.

CONCLUSION

Christianity matters and continues to be a viable resource to navigate people through the vicissitudes of life. Christianity offers a blueprint that explores the spiritual dimension and answers humanities innermost quest for wholeness, purpose and happiness. The aim of this project was to bridge the gap between consistent maturing members, and those who are lost or fallen through the cracks due to shortcomings in the spiritual formation process. I believe that Worship, Discipleship, Fellowship, Ministry and Evangelism are those indispensable factors that would empower believers to live an effective and victorious Christian life. Healthy spiritual formation would circumvent members being lost to a culture of apathy, narcissism and materialism.

Like many believers, I was taught the J-O-Y paradigm. I believe this schematic may predispose one to unhealthy self-care and impede healthy spiritual formation. I believe the spiritual formation process must give careful attention to a process grounded in the development of the self. I believe a developed self through Worship and Discipleship better equip believers to face the harsh realities of life. I believe one's true self is discovered as we take off the 'old skins' and allow ourselves to be transformed through spiritual disciplines and foundational truths. Tier 1 is that viable resource that believers can employ to gain access to the blessed resources that the presence of God provides. Tier 1 affords the freshness of the new wine of the Spirit to pour into our 'new skins.'

Kirk Byron Jones states, "There are many Scripture references, not to mention post-biblical examples that tout personal abandonment as a necessary and continuous act of faithful service. Self-sacrifice is a hallmark of our faith, yet in most of the world's great religions, self-care is an equally essential component of spiritual well-being."[1] I now believe that a healthy spiritual formation model must be grounded in the development of self, before Christian love can be shared to others. "Well-doing, devoid of proper self-care is, at best, doing well poorly. Exemplary care for others is rooted in vigilant self-care."[2] To this end, Tier 1 is a continuous and on-going process.

As believers progress Tier 2 and Tier 3 (to be discussed in Volumes 2 & 3), they must continue to be grounded in Tier 1. I am careful not to confuse development of the self with the narcissistic self-love that has invaded our culture. These are two completely opposing phenomena.

Healthy spiritual formation achieved through a clear and concise Spiritual Formation Model that embodies those indispensable factors for living an effective Christian life is attainable and should be made available by every church entrusted with the souls of men and women. I believe that the Christian Church will thrive and overcome the negativities of the present culture, by providing a healthy and relevant congregational context conducive for healthy and wholesome Christian identity and development. I believe Tier 1 is a framework that could assist in that endeavor.

ENDNOTES

[1]Kirk Byron Jones, 15-16.

[2]Ibid. 8.

TIER 1
AWARDS & HONORS:

Dr. Moody has received the following awards and recognitions for his book: **Shelby County Board of Commissioners Ruby J. Payne Outstanding Author of the Month Award**, Memphis, TN, May 2018; **Certificate of Special Congressional Recognition** – U.S. House of Representatives, Memphis, TN, May 2018; **The Meharry Medical College Recognition**, May 2018; The Newark Municipal Council Resolution, City of Newark, June 2018; Mayor Ras J. Baraka Recognition, Newark, NJ, June 2018; The New Jersey General Assembly Resolution, Trenton, NJ, June 2018; **The U.S. States of Representatives, Certificate of Special Congressional Recognition**, Newark, NJ, June 2018; the Distinguished 2018 ICEA Aida Ford Scholar Winner, Atlanta, GA, August 2018; Region II ICEA Annual Convention, **ICEA Recognition & Presentation**, Tarrytown, NY, September 2018; The New Jersey Performing Arts Center, Authors Forum – featuring Dr. Willie Moody, October 2018; The 2018 Talented Tenth Gala Award Winner, Washington Fisk Alumni Association, October 2018; and The New Jersey District Council of PAW, ICEA **Recognition & Presentation**, Mount laurel, NJ, November 2018.

APPENDIX

THE TERMS

- **Chief Paradigm**: Worship, Ministry, Discipleship, Evangelism, Fellowship - the primary parameters explored for this project. Those Indispensable factors and tenets of the Faith that embrace Spiritual Disciplines inherent for healthy spiritual formation.

- **Worship**: Reverence rendered unto God; a form of religious practice with its creed and ritual.

- **Ministry**: The church's internal mechanisms to minister to one another's needs.

- **Discipleship**: A schematic employed by the ministry to indoctrinate new members with the goal of equipping them for spiritual maturity.

- **Evangelism**: The church's outreach and mission strategies to win souls to Christ; to preach the gospel of Jesus Christ with the goal of conversion.

- **Fellowship**: Community of interest, activity, feeling or experience; the quality or state of being comradely; membership partnership.

- **Disciple**: One who accepts the doctrines of Jesus Christ and assists in spreading this Gospel; a professed follower of Christ.

- **Spiritual Identity**: Full awareness and understanding of the spiritual dimension and benefits/costs of the new birth experience.

- **Spiritual Formation Model**: A schematic that employs spiritual disciplines with the goal of achieving spiritual maturity.

- **Effective Christian Living**: A holistic lifestyle where mind, body and soul are in balance with a realistic understanding of fundamental truths of the faith.

- **Spiritual Disciplines**: Practices like prayer, fasting, devotion, meditation, worship, and singing that enhance the spiritual dimension through consistent praxis.

- **Mission Statement**: The stated goals and objectives of the church with its purpose, scope and strategy.

- **Social Theory of Change**: The underlying motives, principles and guidelines which shapes a ministries global outlook on discipleship and spiritual formation.

CHOSEN GENERATION COMMUNITY CHURCH
"EXPLORING INDISPENSABLE FACTORS IN LIVING AN EFFECTIVE CHRISTIAN LIFE"

SURVEY: THIS ANONYMOUS SURVEY SEEKS TO OBTAIN YOUR OPINION OF THOSE INDISPENSIBLE FACTORS IN LIVING AN EFFECTIVE CHRISTIAN LIFE. THIS IS NOT A DENOMINATIONAL SURVEY POLL. IT DOES NOT ATTEMPT TO EXPLORE OR RATE THE RESPONDENTS RELIGIOUS AFFILIATIONS. THIS INFORMATION WILL BE HELD IN THE STRICTEST OF CONFIDENCE AND USED TO PROVIDE FEEDBACK TO YOUR RELIGIOUS INSTITUTION AND TO DEVELOP A DISCIPLESHIP MODEL TO AID FUTURE CHRISTIANS. FOR ANY 'NO' RESPONSES FEEL FREE TO PROVIDE AN EXPLANATION ON THE BACK OF THIS SURVEY FORM!

AGE: _____   SEX: _____   RACE: _____

1. Were you invited to participate in an **Altar Call** to Discipleship? Yes___ No ___

2. Did you **understand** the Call to Discipleship? Yes ___ No ___

3. Was your **conversion** recognized and/or celebrated by your church? Yes ___ No ___

4. Were you offered a **new members class** at your church? Yes ___ No ___

5. Did this class provide you an understanding of your **new** Christian identity? Yes__No__

6. Were you offered **discipleship lessons** for continued spiritual growth? Yes ___ No ___

7. Did the lessons provide a clear path for **healthy** spiritual development? Yes ___ No ___

8. Did the lessons provide an understanding of the importance of **Worship**? Yes__No___

9. Did the lessons provide an understanding of the importance of **Ministry**? Yes___ No ___

10. Did the lessons provide an understanding of the importance of **Discipleship**? Yes__No__

11. Did the lessons provide an understanding of the importance of **Evangelism**? Yes__No__

12. Did the lessons provide an understanding of the importance of **Fellowship**? Yes__No __

13. Does your church **reach out** to you when you are absent or away? Yes ___ No ___

14. Are you aware of your church's **Mission Statement**? Yes ___ No ___

15. Does your church **do** what the Mission Statement says it will do? Yes ___ No ___

16. Are you living an **effective** Christian life as a result of the lessons offered you? Yes__No_

17. Can you describe **how** the discipleship lessons **improved** your spiritual development?

_____
_____
_____
_____
_____
_____
_____

SURVEY RESULTS

TABLE 1 - Quantitive Breakdown by Churches: Demographics

	Church A	Church B	Church C	Church D
Total	24	24	20	12
Median Age	48	43	44	47
Sex M	7	8	5	7
Sex F	17	16	13	5
Sex NR			2	
Race BLK	24	21	19	9
RaceWHT				2
Race NR		3	1	1

TABLE 2 - Quantitive Breakdown by Churches: Respondent Answers

	Church A			Church B			Church C			Church D		
	Yes	No	NR	Yes	No	NR	Yes	No	NR	Yes	No	NR
1. Were you invited to participate in an **Altar Call** to Discipleship?	19	4	1	19	4	1	20			9	2	1
2. Did you **understand** the Call to Discipleship?	18	6		18	5	1	20			9	3	
3. Was your **conversion** recognized and/or celebrated by your church?	19	4	1	19	5		20			11		1
4. Were you offered a **new members class** at your church?	21	3		12	11		20			8	3	1
5. Did this class provide you an understanding of your **new** Christian identity?	18	5	1	15	7	2	20			10	2	
6. Were you offered **discipleship lessons** for continued spiritual growth?	18	6		20	4		20			9	3	
7. Did the lessons provide a clear path for **healthy** spiritual development?	20	4		20	4		20			11	1	
8. Did the lessons provide an understanding of the importance of **Worship**?	18	5	1	20	4		19		1	11	1	
9. Did the lessons provide an understanding of the importance of **Ministry**?	18	5	1	20	3	1	19		1	10	2	
10. Did the lessons provide an understanding of the importance of **Discipleship**?	15	7	2	18	6		18		2	10	2	
11. Did the lessons provide an understanding of the importance of **Evangelism**?	16	7	1	20	4		18	2		9	3	
12. Did the lessons provide an understanding of the importance of **Fellowship**?	20	3	1	22	2		18		2	11	1	
13. Does your church **reach out** to you when you are absent or away?	14	7	3	19	3	2	20			10	2	
14. Are you aware of your church's **Mission Statement**?	22	1	1	16	8		20			12		
15. Does your church **do** what the Mission Statement says it will do?	21		3	14	7	3	20			12		
16. Are you living an **effective** Christian life as a result of the lessons offered you?	20	1	3	18	6		20			12		

Table 3 - Quantitive Breakdown Grand Total: Demographics

Grand Total	80	
Median Age	46	
Sex M	27	34%
Sex F	51	64%
Sex NR	2	3%
Race BLK	68	85%
Race WHT	2	3%
Race NR	10	22%

Table 4 - Quantitive Breakdown Grand Totals: Respondent Answers

	Total Answers			Percentage		
	Yes	N0	NR	Yes	N0	NR
1. Were you invited to participate in an **Altar Call** to Discipleship?	67	10	3	84%	13%	4%
2. Did you **understand** the Call to Discipleship?	65	15	0	81%	19%	0%
3. Was your **conversion** recognized and/or celebrated by your church?	69	9	2	86%	11%	3%
4. Were you offered a **new members class** at your church?	61	17	2	76%	21%	3%
5. Did this class provide you an understanding of your **new** Christian identity?	63	14	3	79%	18%	4%
6. Were you offered **discipleship lessons** for continued spiritual growth?	67	13	0	84%	16%	0%
7. Did the lessons provide a clear path for **healthy** spiritual development?	71	9	0	89%	11%	0%
8. Did the lessons provide an understanding of the importance of **Worship**?	68	10	2	85%	13%	3%
9. Did the lessons provide an understanding of the importance of **Ministry**?	67	10	3	84%	13%	4%
10. Did the lessons provide an understanding of the importance of **Discipleship**?	61	15	4	76%	19%	5%
11. Did the lessons provide an understanding of the importance of **Evangelism**?	63	16	1	79%	20%	1%
12. Did the lessons provide an understanding of the importance of **Fellowship**?	71	6	3	89%	8%	4%
13. Does your church **reach out** to you when you are absent or away?	63	12	5	79%	15%	6%
14. Are you aware of your church's **Mission Statement**?	70	9	1	88%	11%	1%
15. Does your church **do** what the Mission Statement says it will do?	67	7	6	84%	9%	8%
16. Are you living an **effective** Christian life as a result of the lessons offered you?	70	7	3	88%	9%	4%

BIBLIOGRAPHY

Ackerman, John. *Spiritual Awakening: A Guide to Spiritual Life in Congregations*. Colorado Springs, CO: NavPress, 1993.
Anonymous. DMIN Project Survey. 2014.

Arn, Win and Charles Arn. *The Master's Plan for Making Disciples*. Grand Rapids, Michigan: Baker Books, 1998.

Arthur, Sarah. *Credo: faith formation for older youth and young adults*. Nashville, TN: Cokesbury, 2012.

Augsburger, David. *Dissident Discipleship: A Spirituality of Self-Surrender, Love of God, and Love of Neighbor*. Grand Rapids, Michigan: Brazos Press, 2006.

Best, Ernest. *Disciples and Discipleship: Studies in the Gospel According to Mark*. Edinburgh, UK: T & T Clark LTD, 1986.

Bradfield, William. *Personality and Fellowship*. London: CH Kelly, 1914.

Brown, David. *Discipleship and Imagination: Christian Tradition and Truth*. Oxford: Oxford University Press, 2000.

Bustraan, Richard. *The Jesus People Movement: A Story of Spiritual Revolution among the Hippies*. Eugene, Oregon: Pickwick Publications, 2014.

Casteel, John. *Spiritual Renewal Through Personal Groups*. New York: Association Press, 1957.

Casteel, John L. ed. *The Creative Role of Interpersonal Groups in the Church Today*. New York: Association Press, 1968.

Cimino, Richard. *Trusting the Spirit: Renewal and Reform in American Religion*. San Francisco: Jossey-Bass, Inc., 2001.

City of Plainfield Website. Accessed October 22, 2014. www.Plainfield.com.

Clark, Freddy James. *Hospitality: An Ecclesiology Practice of Ministry*. Lanham, Maryland: Hamilton Books, 2007.

Dallos, Rudi. *Attachment Narrative Therapy: Integrating Narrative, Systemic and Attachment Therapies*. New York, NY: Open University Press, 2006.

Ecklund, Elaine Howard. *Korean American Evangelicals: New Models for Civic Life*. Oxford: Oxford University Press, 2006.

Edge, Findley B. *A Quest For Vitality in Religion: A Theological Approach to Religious Education*. Nashville, Tennessee: Broadman Press, 1963.

Edge, Findley B. *The Greening of the Church*. Waco, Texas: Word Books Publisher, 1971.

Fenning, Esther Talbout. "Charismatic Renewal: Movement in Worship." *St. Louis Post Dispatch*, Accessed August19, 1994. http://search.proquest.com.ezproxy.drew.edu.

Foster, Richard J. *Sanctuary of the Soul: Journey into Meditative Prayer*. Downers Grove, Illinois: InterVarsity Press Books. 2011.

Foster, Richard J. *Celebration of Discipline: The Path to Spiritual Growth*. San Francisco, CA: Harper & Row Publishers, 1988.

Frawley, PJ. "The Validity of Self-Report Data." *Journal of Alcohol* 48, no. 5 (1988): 263-92.

Gilbert P. John ed, Theresa Gilbert, Patty Johansen and Jay Regenniter. *Charting the Course: A Workbook on Christian Discipleship*. Nashville, Tenn: Discipleship Resources, 2007.

Greenleaf, Robert. *The Servant leader*. Indianapolis, IN: Robert Greenleaf Center, 1991.

Halaas, M.D., Gwen Wagstrom. *The Right Road: Life Choices for Clergy*. Minneapolis, MN: Augsburg Fortress, 2004.

Happel, Stephen and James J. Walter. *Conversion and Discipleship: A Christian Foundation for Ethics and Doctrine*. Philadelphia, PA: Fortress Press, 1986.

Helminiak, Daniel A. *Spiritual Development: An Interdisciplinary Study*. Chicago, Illinois: Loyola University Press, 1997.

Hinton, Jeanne. *Walking in the Same Direction: A New Way of Being Church*. Geneva, Switzerland: World Council of Churches, 1995.

Holmes, Urban T. *Turning to Christ: A Theology of Renewal and Evangelization*. New York: Seabury Press, 1981.

Hughes, Graham. *Worship as Meaning: A Liturgical Theology for Late Modernity*. United Kingdom: Cambridge University Press, 2003.

Johnson, Suzanne. *Christian Spiritual Formation in the Church and Classroom*. Nashville, TN: Abingdon Press, 1989.

Jones, Kirk Byron, *Rest in the Storm: Self-Care Strategies for Clergy and Other Caregivers*. Valley Forge, PA: Judson Press, 2001.

Kelhoffer, James A. *Persecution, Persuasion, and Power: readiness to withstand hardship as a corroboration of legitimacy in the New Testament*. Tubingen: Mohr Siebeck, 2010.

Kemp, Charles F. ed, "The Pastoral Care Movement: A product of many Contributors." *Pastoral Psychology* 18, no. 175 (June 1967): 29 -44.

Kettering, Keith. *The Sanctification Connection: An Exploration of Human Participation in Spiritual Growth*. Lanham, Maryland: University Press of America, 2008.

Labanow, Cory E. *Evangelism and the Emerging Church: A congregational Study of a Vineyard Church*. VT: Ashgate, 2009.

Lamoureux, Patricia. T*he Christian Moral life: Faithful Discipleship for a Global Society*. Maryknoll, NY: Orbis Books, 2010.

Marcoux, Marcene. *Cursillo Anatomy Of A Movement: The Experience of Spiritual Renewal*. New York: Lambeth Press, 1982.

Matthaei, Sondra Higgins. *Formation in Faith: The Congregational Ministry of Making Disciples*. Nashville: Abingdon, 2008.

McGaravan, Donald. *Understanding Church Growth- Fully Revised* Grand Rapids, Michigan: William B. Eerdmans Publishing, 1980.

McGaravan, Donald ed. *Eye of the Storm: The Great Debate in Mission* Waco, Texas: Word Books Publisher, 1972.

McGaravan, Donald, and George G. Hunter III. *Church Growth Strategie That Work. Creative Leadership Series*. Nashville: Abingdon Press, 1980.

Mickey, Paul, Gary Gamble and Paula Gilbert. *Pastoral Assertiveness: A New Model for Pastoral Care.* Nashville: Abingdon, 1978.

Miller, Donald E. *Reinventing American Protestantism: Christianity in the New Millennium.* Berkeley, Calif: Univ of California Press, 1997.

Moore, James W. *Jesus' Parables about Discipleship.* Nashville, TN: Abingdon Press, 2009.

Newby, James R. Elton *Trueblood: Believer, Teacher and Friend.* New York: Harper & Row Publishers, 1990.

Noll, Mark A. *Turning Points: Decisive Moments in the History of Christianity.* Grand Rapids, Michigan: Baker Academic, 2000.

O'Connor, Edward D. ed. *Perspectives on Charismatic Renewal.* Notre Dame, London: University of Notre Dame Press, 1975.

Pak, Ung Kyu. *Asian Thought and Culture: Millennialism in the Korean Protestant Church.* New York: Peter Lang Publishing, Inc., 2005.

Patton, John. *From Ministry to Theology: Pastoral Action & Reflection.* Nashville: Abingdon Press, 1990.

Peterson, Eugene H. *A long Obedience in the Same Direction.* Downers Grove, Illinois: InterVarsity Press, 2000.

Pew Research Center. *"Is Religion's Declining Influence Good or Bad? Those without Religious Affiliation are Divided."Accessed* September 23, 2014, http://www.pewresearch.org/fact-tank/2014/09/23/is-religions-declining-influence-good-or-bad-those-without-religious-affiliation-are-divided.

Quinn, Frederick. Building the "Goodly Fellowship of Faith:" A History of the Episcopal Church in Utah, 1867 – 1996. Logan, Utah: Utah State University Press, 2004.

Redman, Robb. *The Great Worship Awakening: Singing a New Song in the Postmodern Church.* San Francisco, CA: Jossey-Bass Publishers, 2002.

Richardson, Ronald. *Creating a Healthier Church: Family Systems Theory, Leadership, and Congregational Life.* Minneapolis, MN: Fortress Press, 1996.

Richardson, Ronald. *Creating a Healthier Pastor: Family Systems Theory and the Pastor's own Family.* Minneapolis, MN: Augsburg Fortress Press, 2005.

Root, Andrew. *The promise of Despair: the way of the Cross as the way of the Church*. Nashville, TN: Abingdon Press, 2010.

Rusch, William G. *Ecumenism - A Movement Toward Church Unity*. Philadelphia: Fortress Press, 1985.

Seamands, Stephen. *Ministry in the Image of God*. Downers Grove, Illinois: IVP Books, 2005.

Senn, Frank C. *Protestant Spiritual Traditions*. New York: Paulist Press, 1986.

Shaw, Mark. *10 Great Ideas from Church History: A Decision-Maker's Guide to Shaping Your Church*. Downers Grove, Illinois: InterVarsity Press, 1997.

Smail, Tom, Andrew Walker and Nigel Wright. *Charismatic Renewal: The Search for Theology*. Great Britain: Society for Promoting Christian Knowledge, 1995.

Smart, Ninian. *The Concept of Worship*. Macmillan: St. Martin's Press, 1972.

Smith, David. *Mission After Christendom*. London: Darton, Longman & Todd LTD, 2003.

Smith, James K A. *Desiring the Kingdom: Worship, Worldview, and Cultural Formation*. Grand Rapids, MI: Baker Academics, 2009.

Smith, Nathan Delynn. *Roots, Renewal and the Brethren*. Pasenda, CA Hope Publishing House, 1986.

Stone, Howard W. ed. *Strategies For Brief Pastoral Counseling* Minneapolis, MN: Fortress Press, 2001.

Trueblood, D. Elton. *Essays in Gratitude*. Nashville, TN: Broadman Press 1982.

Trueblood, Elton. *While It Is Day: An Autobiography*. New York: Harper & Row Publishers, 1974.

Turner, John G. *Bill Bright & Campus Crusade for Christ: The Renewal of Evangelicalism in Postwar America*. Chapel Hill: The University of North Carolina Press, 2008.

Tuttle, Robert G. *Can We Talk: Sharing Your Faith in a Pre-Christian World*. Nashville: Abingdon Press, 1999.

Villafane, Eldin. *Beyond Cheap grace: A call to Radical Discipleship, Incarnation, and Justice*. Grand Rapids, Michigan: William B. Eerdsman Pub, 2006.

Wagner, C. Peter. *Latin American Theology: Radical or Evangelical?* Grand Rapids, Michigan: William B. Eerdmans Publishing, 1970.

Wagner, C. Peter. *Your Spiritual Gifs Can help Your Church Grow*. Glendale, CA: Regal Books Division, 1974.

Wakefield, Gordon S. *An Outline of Christian Worship*. Edinburgh, Scotland: T & T Clark LTD, 1998.

Wallace, Jim,ed. *The Rise of Christian Conscience: The Emergence of a Dramatic Renewal Movement in the Church Today*. San Francisco: Harper & Row Publishers, 1987.

Warren, Rick. *The Purpose Driven Church: Growth Without Compromising Your Message & Mission*. Grand Rapids, MI: Zondervan, 1995.

Warren, Rick. *The Purpose Driven Life: What on Earth Am I Here For?* Grand Rapids, MI: Zondervan, 2002.

Weems Jr., Lovett H. and Tom Berlin. *Bearing Fruit: Ministry With Real Results*. Nashville: Abingdon Press, 2011.

Wilhoit, James C. *Spiritual Formation as if the Church Mattered: Growing n Christ through Community*. Grand Rapids, Michigan: Baker Academic, 2008.

Willard, Dallas. *The Divine Conspiracy: Rediscovering Our Hidden Life in God*. San Francisco, CA: Harper Collins Publisher. 1998.

Wise, Carroll A. *The Meaning of Pastoral Care*. New York: Harper & Row Publishers, 1966.

World Council of Churches. *Voices Of Solidarity: A Story of Christian ay Centres, Academies and Movements For Social Concern*, Geneva, Switzerland: World Council of Churches, 1981.

Worley, Robert C. *A Gathering Of Strangers: Understanding The Life Of Your Church*. Philadelphia, PA: Westminster Press, 1976.

Yoo, Boo-Woong. *Korean Pentecostalism Its History and Theology*. Frankfurt am Main: Verlag Peter Lang, 1988.

Yust, Karen-Marie. *Taught by God: Teaching and Spiritual Formation*. St. Louis, MO: Chalice Press, 2006.

Ziegler, Edward K. *"Nurture of the Church through Group Life." Brethren Life and Thought 6, no. 4* (September 1, 1961): 37-46. Accessed November 18, 2014. http://ezproxy.drew.edu/login?url=http://search.ebscohost.com/login.aspx?direct=true&db=rfh&AN=ATLA0000680117&site=ehost-live&scope=site

TIER 1:
DISCOVERING SELF
"NEW WINE, OLD SKINS"

REVISED EDITION

centralagnewark@yahoo.com
www.chosencc.wix.com/chosengenerationcc

Made in the USA
Middletown, DE
15 October 2021

49853143R00076